103 FUN WAYS TO ENJOY RETIREMENT LIKE A QUEEN

*A Unique Gift for Women
Who Refuse to Be Ordinary*

REBEL BOOMERS INK

TABLE OF CONTENTS

Introduction... 5

Retirement isn't the end—it's the beginning of your boldest chapter yet.

Chapter 1: Bye Bye Boredom, Hello Fun!............................... 9

Because beige cardigans are optional, but fun is not.

Chapter 2: Rebel Against Stereotypes 25

Break every rule about what retirement "should" look like.

Chapter 3: The Queen of Social Life 41

Your new social calendar is about to get fabulous.

Chapter 4: Revenge of the Bucket List—Doing What You Never Had Time to Do 57

All those dreams you didn't have time for? It's time.

Chapter 5: I'm Not Dead, I'm Just Getting Started—Redefining What Retirement Looks Like.. 73

Because slowing down is overrated—and you're just warming up.

Chapter 6: Hobbies That Won't Bore You to Death (Literally)......... 91

From fire dancing to axe throwing—yes, really.

Chapter 7: The "Why the Hell Not?" Challenge – Saying Yes to the Unexpected... 109

Say yes to the wild, the weird, and the wonderfully unexpected.

Chapter 8: Badass Career Changes– Because You're Not Done Yet 127

New jobs. New passions. No business suits required.

Chapter 9: How to Travel Without Children and Enjoy It 145

Jet-set your way—no snacks, no tantrums, all freedom.

Conclusion: Long Live the Queen (That's You) 163

References 166

Look at you—bold, brilliant, and unstoppable. Crown on.

© Copyright 2025 - All rights reserved.

The content contained within this book may not be reproduced, duplicated or transmitted without direct written permission from the author or the publisher.

Under no circumstances will any blame or legal responsibility be held against the publisher, or author, for any damages, reparation, or monetary loss due to the information contained within this book, either directly or indirectly.

Legal Notice:

This book is copyright protected. It is only for personal use. You cannot amend, distribute, sell, use, quote or paraphrase any part, or the content within this book, without the consent of the author or publisher.

Disclaimer Notice:

Please note the information contained within this document is for educational and entertainment purposes only. All effort has been executed to present accurate, up to date, reliable, complete information. No warranties of any kind are declared or implied. Readers acknowledge that the author is not engaged in the rendering of legal, financial, medical or professional advice. The content within this book has been derived from various sources. Please consult a licensed professional before attempting any techniques outlined in this book.

By reading this document, the reader agrees that under no circumstances is the author responsible for any losses, direct or indirect, that are incurred as a result of the use of the information contained within this document, including, but not limited to, errors, omissions, or inaccuracies.

INTRODUCTION

Let's get one thing straight: You did not work your entire adult life just to be handed a pair of fuzzy slippers and a book on how to crochet. No ma'am, not today, not ever! You are not a human relic meant to spend your golden years babysitting grandkids, knitting scarves, and eating dinner in front of the television, just to fall asleep before 7 p.m. You've spent decades answering to alarms, deadlines, and bosses. Now that you've finally broken free, society expects you to slow down and "take it easy?" Ha! I say, let's take retirement and turn it into the best chapter yet—one filled with adventure, laughter, and doing whatever the heck you want!

Meet Christine: The Rebel Retiree We All Need

Christine gets it. She spent 27 years as a nurse, putting everyone else's needs first. The moment she clocked out of her last shift, she felt freer than any woman who's ever taken off her bra after a 14-hour day. Her husband threw her a retirement party—adorable, right? But she wasn't prepared for the gifts. Warm cardigans, heating pads, a brand new recliner, and so many books to help her "relax and read." What on earth? She wasn't moving into a retirement village; she was just getting started!

So, she made an announcement. "Can I have your attention, please!" she said, commanding the room. Christine thanked everyone for coming and then dropped the bombshell: She was taking a golden gap year. No obligations. No schedules. Just pure, unfiltered, do-what-the-heck-I-want time. The next thing her family knew, she and her husband were off on a year-long adventure. More salsa dancing, fewer slippers. More cobblestone streets in Europe, fewer evenings dozing off at 6 p.m. More sunsets in the Sahara while riding a camel, fewer Netflix marathons. Christine wasn't retiring from life, she was finally living it.

Christine isn't an anomaly; she's a pioneer. And now, it's your turn. Welcome to the rebellious retiree mindset, where we rewrite the outdated script on what retirement is supposed to look like. This mindset is built on three golden principles:

1. Eliminate the words "too late" from your vocabulary. There's no expiration date on fun. If you've ever thought, *I wish I did that when I was younger*, guess what? You can still do it now!

2. Step outside your comfort zone. Retirement is the time to do the things that set your soul on fire. Try, fail, laugh, repeat.

3. Shock at least one person a month. Nothing says "I'm still kicking" like doing something that makes people say, "You did WHAT?!" Take a pole dancing class, go skydiving, adopt a pet iguana—whatever makes your heart race.

This book is not just a list of cute ideas. As you turn these pages, you'll find 103 ideas to make retirement the adventure of a lifetime—some practical (but still exciting), some outrageous. Either way, they're all designed to inspire you to embrace this stage with open arms and a fearless heart.

So, what dreams have you shelved over the years? Dust them off. Make a list. Let's get to work crafting your own rebel wishlist, the things you've always wanted to do but never made time for. This is *your* time, and trust me, it's going to be spectacular.

Let's do this!

CHAPTER 1:

BYE BYE BOREDOM, HELLO FUN!

Okay, let's get one thing straight: Retirement is not some slow fade into boredom and beige cardigans. This is your chance to rewrite the rules, toss the schedule, and finally stop pretending you enjoy predictable dinner routines and early bedtimes (unless you actually do, in which case, carry on).

This chapter is all about having fun. The kind that makes you laugh so hard you snort, the kind that gives you stories your grandkids will definitely roll their eyes at someday. Because truth be told, retirement should never be framed at your end. It's your beautiful beginning of adventures, hobbies, wild ideas, and a little harmless mischief.

We're ditching the "I don't know what to do with myself" vibes and diving headfirst into exciting, creative ways to kick off this chapter of your life with confidence, curiosity, and yes, plenty of fun.

Ready? Good. Let's show boredom the door.

Write Your Rebel Wishlist
Things You've Never Dared to Try

It's time to toss aside that boring bucket list and craft your very own *rebel wishlist*. This is a unique, no-limits lineup of everything you've secretly dreamed of but never dared to try and likely never had the time to pursue. Remember all those meetings, obligations, and rigid schedules that have always stood in your way? Well, now nothing is off-limits! Grab a pen and paper and write it all down. Yes, every single wild idea! At no point should you hesitate and think to yourself, *Oh my gosh, I couldn't possibly*. You absolutely can, and you absolutely should! Once your wishlist is complete, consider sharing it with a friend or two for accountability. You might even find someone who is eager to join you on this thrilling adventure. Keep this list dynamic by adding, tweaking, or dreaming even bigger. Your goal is to rediscover what makes you giddy; this is your life's encore, so make it as wild and wonderful as you desire!

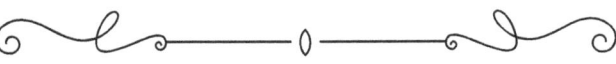

Throw a Retirement Party With a Surprise Theme

Everyone Comes in Costume

Who says retirement parties have to be boring or predictable? Not us! Give yourself permission to throw a themed bash where costumes are nonnegotiable. Picture a cool "Wild West" showdown, a hilarious "Famous Duos" night, or a nostalgic "Decades You Barely Survived" celebration. The goal? Pure fun, laughter, and memories that stick. Spice things up with a costume contest and don't hold back on the outrageous prizes. After all, nothing brings people together like battling it out for a rhinestone-studded tiara or a gold spray-painted trophy. Just imagine the moment your quiet accountant walks in dressed as Dolly Parton, absolutely priceless! This is your moment to shine, so why not embrace the joy, the ridiculousness, and the sparkle? Retirement is a milestone worth celebrating with flair, laughter, and just a hint of mischief. Go all out and make it a night everyone will remember and laugh about long after the last piece of cake is gone.

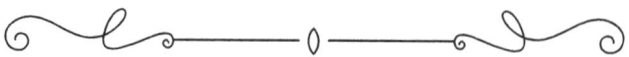

Try Your Hand at Street Art
Leave a Colorful Mark on the City

Why not trade your to-do list for a can of spray paint and leave your mark, literally? Street art isn't just for 20-somethings with hoodies and headphones; it's a vibrant choice by artists of all ages, backgrounds, and experiences. Whether it's murals, chalk art, or stenciling, find your vibe and let your creativity loose in your community. In cities like Berlin, with its famous East Side Gallery, or Banksy's iconic works in London, the streets are galleries filled with stories waiting to be told. And guess what? No one cares if you color outside the lines anymore; in fact, it's encouraged! Join a local art project or workshop. Check out organizations like the Mural Arts Program in Philadelphia or local initiatives in your city where you might connect with fellow creative souls (Home - Mural Arts, 2025). You could even meet your new bestie while painting a giant sunflower on a brick wall. It's bold, it's beautiful, and it's your chance to say, "I was here" in the most colorful way possible. Remember, art can transform spaces and communities, making them more vibrant and alive.

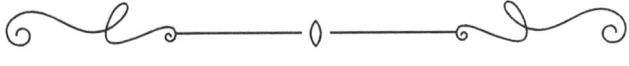

Create a Passions Jar
Fill It With Spontaneous Adventure Ideas

Meet your new partner in adventure: the passions jar! All you need is a simple jar and some colorful paper. Start writing down every fun, quirky, or exciting activity you've ever dreamed of trying, big or small. Maybe it's signing up for a pottery class, belting your heart out at karaoke, joining a salsa dancing lesson, or exploring a local hiking trail. Whenever boredom creeps in or you're craving a new experience, pull a slip from the jar and dive right in. Want to level it up? Invite friends or family to add their own ideas because nothing bonds people faster than an unexpected round of goat yoga or a spontaneous road trip. The magic of the passions jar lies in its simplicity—no overthinking or endless planning required, just pure, ready-to-go inspiration. Retirement isn't about slowing down; it's your time to play, explore, and say yes to every adventure waiting around the corner!

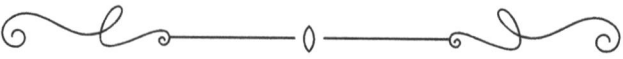

Sign Up for an Improv Acting Class

Embrace Spontaneity and Laughter

Ready to laugh so hard you snort? Improv acting classes might just be your new favorite adventure and the perfect cure for that annoying *"I have to get it right"* mindset. Improv invites you to step into a world of spontaneity, creativity, and pure fun. Legendary spots like The Second City in Chicago or Upright Citizens Brigade in New York City offer classes that sharpen your quick thinking, boost adaptability, and, best of all, help you find humor in just about anything. You'll also build confidence for those real-life "what do I say now?" moments, whether you're making small talk at a party, navigating a networking event, or just trying to survive a family gathering. Plus, you'll meet fellow fun-seekers ready to embrace the ridiculous because nothing bonds people faster than silly impersonations, hilarious scenes, and belly laughs. So, why not give it a shot? Improv is a thrilling way to say yes to new experiences—and you'll leave every class grinning.

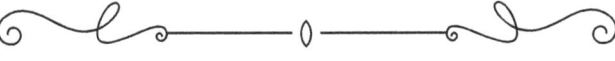

Take Up Sand Art Sculpting
Build Massive, Intricate Sandcastles

Who says sandcastles are just for kids? It's time to grab your sunscreen, roll up your sleeves, and channel your inner artist with a day of sand sculpting fun. Whether you're crafting towering castles worthy of a contest or sculpting sea creatures inspired by the incredible Sand Sculpture Festival in Blankenberge, Belgium, sand art is the perfect mix of creativity, relaxation, and pure joy. Make it even more memorable by inviting friends, family, or grandkids for a friendly competition—the winner gets treated to ice cream! And don't worry if there's no beach nearby—your backyard or a local park with a sandbox works just as well. It's less about location and more about letting your imagination run wild. The best part? Every tide—or even a quick rinse with the hose—clears your canvas, inviting you to create again. So go ahead, embrace the magic of sand sculpting. This is what retirement should feel like—playful, creative, and full of simple pleasures.

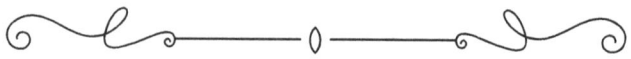

Master the Art of Illusions and Magic Tricks
Perform at Local Events

Why not add a little mystery and magic to your retirement by learning the art of illusions? Mastering a few card tricks, sleight-of-hand moves, or even mind-reading stunts is a fun way to surprise others—and nothing lights up a room like making someone's watch disappear. But magic isn't just for kids' birthday parties; it's an impressive skill that sharpens your mind, boosts your confidence, and guarantees you'll be the most unforgettable guest at any gathering. You can even take a class at a local community center or check out a specialty school like The Magic Castle in Los Angeles, which offers workshops for aspiring magicians. Prefer learning from home? Explore online platforms like MasterClass, where legends like Penn & Teller teach their secrets. Or dive into YouTube tutorials to practice tricks at your own pace. Either way, adding a little magic to your life is a fantastic way to stay sharp, have fun, and keep everyone guessing what you'll do next!

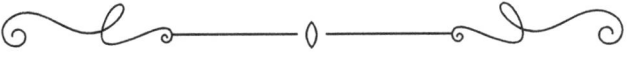

ENJOY RETIREMENT LIKE A QUEEN

Become a Flamenco or Bollywood Dancer

Dive Into Cultural Dance

Nothing shakes off the ordinary quite like learning a dance style that's anything but basic. Imagine diving into flamenco, with its fiery footwork, passionate rhythms, and dramatic flair—instantly transporting you to the heart of Spain. Or embrace the vibrant, high-energy world of Bollywood dance, where every move feels straight out of a colorful film like *Dil Se* or *Lagaan*. Both styles offer more than just great exercise—they're an immersive cultural experience that connects you with music, tradition, and new people. Join a local dance studio like DanceWithMe in New York or explore vibrant dance communities through platforms like Meetup, where workshops and events are always happening nearby. You might even find yourself attending incredible festivals like the Madrid Flamenco Festival or the International Bollywood Dance Festival, where the energy is absolutely contagious. Dancing isn't just movement—it's expression, connection, and joy. So, why not step outside your comfort zone, learn something new, and feel truly alive while doing it?

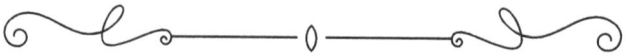

Study Professional Poker or Blackjack Strategy

Compete in Vegas Tournaments

Why not make your next trip to Vegas interesting and maybe even profitable? Learning the strategy behind poker or blackjack transforms gambling into a legitimate mental workout. It's a blend of skill, psychology, and mastering a killer poker face (sunglasses optional). Consider exploring books like *The Theory of Poker* by David Sklansky or taking online courses from sites like MasterClass, where you can learn from experts like Phil Ivey. Local meetups or game nights, often advertised on platforms like Meetup.com, can provide hands-on experience to sharpen your strategy. Once you feel confident, hit the tables at iconic venues like the Bellagio or the Venetian and test your skills in a real tournament. Win or lose, you'll undoubtedly have a blast and probably some wild stories to share. Plus, retirement's the perfect time to relish the experience of sitting at a table where bluffing is a skill, not a social faux pas. Please play responsibly.

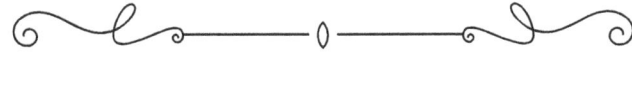

Join a Professional Flash Mob
Surprise Performances in Public Places

Are you ready to channel your inner performer and shock a few strangers in the best way possible? Joining a professional flash mob is pure adrenaline-fueled fun. One minute, you're blending in like everyone else waiting for your coffee at Starbucks, and the next, you're breaking into a choreographed dance in the middle of a bustling mall, a sunny park such as Golden Gate Park, or a bustling train station reminiscent of Grand Central Terminal. It's unexpected, it's hilarious, and honestly, it's unforgettable. Flash mobs are the perfect mix of creativity, community, and "what did I just witness?" energy. This is a great opportunity to meet fellow adventurers who aren't afraid to dance like everyone's watching because they totally are. How do you find flash mobs to join? Check out websites like Flash Mob America or Improv Everywhere. They offer insights and opportunities to join in on this exhilarating experience.

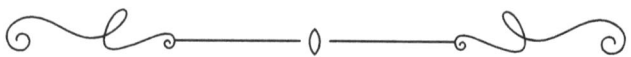

Host a Pop-Up Themed Dinner in a Mystery Location

Why not turn dinner into an adventure? Plan a pop-up themed dinner party, but here's the twist: guests only get the theme (think Parisian Café Night or Tropical Luau) and a meeting point. The actual dinner spot? A secret until they arrive, adding an element of surprise. Picture a cozy backyard illuminated with fairy lights, a vibrant rooftop overlooking the city skyline, or a serene beach under the moonlight. Why not include costumes, music, and over-the-top decorations? Whether it's the whimsy of a vintage train car reminiscent of The Orient Express or the charm of a secret garden inspired by Alice in Wonderland, the possibilities are endless. It's part mystery, part culinary adventure, and all unforgettable. Plus, nothing beats watching friends' faces light up when they realize they're dining under the stars or surrounded by lush tropical décor. Consider checking out Airbnb Experiences, where unique dining experiences are offered. Retirement's new motto? If you're going to eat dinner, make it an event.

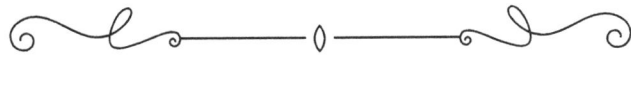

Meet Gloria: The Day a Retired Queen Wrote Her Rebel Wishlist and Shocked Her Bridge Club

Gloria had done everything "right" her whole life. Married at 22. Raised three kids, each with dental work straight out of an orthodontist's dream. Retired from her library job with a pension, a gold watch, and the quiet admiration of the entire Friends of the Library committee.

But two months into retirement, Gloria was restless. The days stretched wide—too wide. After one too many afternoons rearranging her spice rack alphabetically and by heat level, she stumbled upon a podcast called "Rebel Women Over 60" (because of course that exists, and it's fabulous). The host? A sassy Brit named Margo who casually mentioned something called a Rebel Wishlist (Sellwood, 2025).

It wasn't a bucket list. This was about the things you always secretly wanted to do but didn't because life, kids, mortgages, or your mother's voice whispering, "That's not ladylike, dear" got in the way.

Gloria poured a glass of merlot, grabbed her leopard print journal (a gift from her wildest friend, Brenda), and started writing:

- ◊ Get a tattoo.
- ◊ Try pole dancing.
- ◊ Visit Iceland and sit in a hot spring naked.
- ◊ Audition for community theater.
- ◊ Eat gelato in Florence.

- ◊ Crash a bachelorette party.
- ◊ Learn to drive a motorcycle.

She stared at the list, laughed… and texted her friend Brenda: "You busy next week? I'm getting a tattoo."

The following Wednesday, Gloria and Brenda walked into a local spot known for being "senior-friendly" (read: no judgment, lots of numbing cream). The tattoo artist, a bearded 20-something named Kai, blinked twice when Gloria confidently handed over a sketch of a queen's crown with the word "Fearless" beneath it.

"First tattoo?" he asked.

"First rebellion," Gloria smirked.

One hour later, Gloria strutted out of the shop with a bandaged wrist, texting a photo to her bridge group. "Your move, ladies."

The Wrap-Up: Ready for What's Next?

See? Boredom doesn't stand a chance when you're busy building sandcastles, mastering card tricks, and flash-mobbing your way through retirement. These ideas are about living it up and creating stories you'll be laughing about for years and possibly oversharing at family gatherings.

This is only the beginning. Next up, we're really turning up the heat. Get ready to rebel against every tired stereotype about what retirement should look like. It's time to color outside the lines, shake things up, and prove that adventure doesn't have an expiration date. Let's go!

CHAPTER 2

REBEL AGAINST STEREOTYPES

Let's be real: Retirement isn't your cue to shrink, slow down, or start collecting cat figurines (unless you really love cats, of course). It's time to flip the script on every tired stereotype about what retired women are "supposed" to do because nobody gets to decide that but you.

This chapter gives you a road map on how to go full rebel mode. We're talking thrills, adventures, and those wild, head-turning moments that make people say, "Wait... she did WHAT?" You've earned the right to live boldly, so let's dive into 11 daring ideas guaranteed to make retirement your most exciting chapter yet.

Become a Storm Chaser
Join a Meteorology Team and Witness Nature's Fury Up Close

Ditch the weather apps and dive straight into the heart of nature's fury with a storm-chasing adventure! Join a professional team from places like storm-chasing.com, and become the ultimate storm tracker, hunting down tornadoes, electric lightning storms, and swirling clouds like a true daredevil. It's a wild mix of science and adrenaline that'll make even your wildest bingo stories sound tame. Not only will you gather wildly entertaining tales, but you'll also pick up some crazy meteorology skills along the way. Imagine the thrill of standing right in the middle of a storm, feeling the sheer power of Mother Nature. Then, the next time someone casually asks what you've been up to, you can lean back and say, "Oh, just chasing storms." It's a total mic-drop moment. Who said thrill-seeking is just for the young, right? Storm chasing is for anyone ready to welcome and accept their inner adventurer! It's time to get ready for an experience that's downright electrifying!

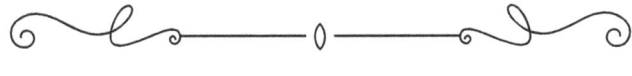

RACE CARS AT A PROFESSIONAL TRACK
Learn to Drive Like a Pro

Ready to swap the family minivan for a beast that purrs with power? Why not enroll in an exhilarating racing course at top-notch venues like the Skip Barber Racing School or Bondurant racing school to conquer those thrilling curves, leave your mark on the asphalt, and savor the pure adrenaline of the track? You'll suit up in a stylish racing outfit, ignite the engine, and finally answer the burning question: What if I had chased my dream of becoming a racecar driver? I'm here to remind you that it's never too late! Whether you dive into Formula One racing, tackle stock cars, or dive headfirst into the heart-pounding world of drag racing, you'll leave behind the stereotypes, and anyone else chasing your tail. Plus, your daily ride will feel like an epic race; watch out, Grandma! And retirement? Toss aside that speed limit; the only limit here is your zest for adventure. So, fasten your seatbelt and prepare to revamp your life story!

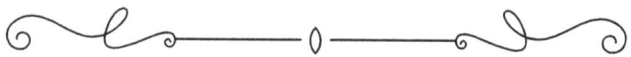

Live on a Boat for a Year
Sail the World or Hug the Coastline

Have you ever fantasized about trading your mundane land life for the thrill of the open sea? Why not turn your retirement into the ultimate escapade by living on a boat for an entire year? Can you imagine yourself breezing through the Caribbean or hugging the coastlines of California, where every sunrise paints a masterpiece across the horizon, and each night cradles you to sleep like your favorite lullaby? You'll pick up essential navigation and marine skills, and who knows, you might even discover your sea legs or develop an affectionate bond with dock life. You can wake up to the playful antics of dolphins instead of the dreaded hum of a neighbor's lawn mower. That is what I call pure bliss! Websites like sailaway.co can help you find your perfect vessel while resources like the "Boat and Breakfast" directory will turn any port into your next adventure hub. This is your year to float, explore, and pen your most riveting chapters yet. Leave behind the ordinary and embrace the extraordinary, you won't regret it!

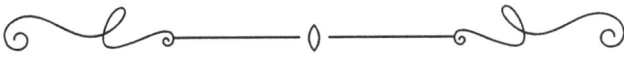

Join an Archaeological Dig
Help Unearth History in Exotic Locations

Why limit yourself to reading about ancient civilizations when you can excavate them? Why not sign up for an archaeological dig and immerse yourself in the dirt of history? Whether you find yourself unearthing treasures in Greece, Egypt, or even an undiscovered gem near your hometown, you'll master excavation techniques while channeling your inner Indiana Jones, fedora completely optional! The excitement of discovery is unparalleled. Imagine uncovering something that hasn't seen the light of day for millennia! Plus, you'll meet fellow enthusiasts who share your passion for dirt and hidden secrets. Forget the notion that retirement means stagnant pursuits; it's your chance to uncover the captivating tales buried right beneath your feet, one enthusiastic trowel at a time. Websites like Archaeological.org and Earthwatch.org offer opportunities to join digs and dive into history. So roll up your sleeves, grab a shovel, and prepare for the adventure of a lifetime! Who knew retirement could be so exhilarating? Let the treasure hunting begin!

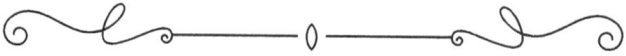

16

Become a Paranormal Investigator

Hunt for Ghosts in Haunted Locations

Have you always had a thing for the creepy, mysterious, and eerie? Now's the perfect time to dive in and become a paranormal investigator! Picture yourself exploring haunted mansions like the Winchester Mystery House, eerie cemeteries such as Greyfriars Kirkyard, or ghost-infested hotels like the Stanley Hotel. With electromagnetic field detectors in hand and curiosity fueling your adventures, you'll be on a spirited quest to uncover the supernatural while crafting spine-tingling tales to share with friends. Whether you capture proof of a ghostly presence or just get a spine-tingling thrill, each expedition will leave you with unforgettable memories. Plus, ghost hunts make a way more exciting alternative to yet another dull coffee meetup. Who knew retirement could mean trading in your knitting needles for night-vision goggles and electronic voice phenomenon recordings? Remember, you'll never have a dull moment when you're chasing shadows and unearthing stories from the other side! Check out websites like Ghost Hunters or Local Ghost Tours to jump-start your ghost-busting journey.

Get a Pilot's License
Fly a Plane and Explore the Skies

Why stay earthbound when you can literally soar? Earning your pilot's license transforms the vast sky into your personal playground. You can be the one flying over the Statue of Liberty or cruising above the Golden Gate Bridge, all while feeling the exhilarating rush of takeoff. It's not just a thrill; it's a superpower. You'll master navigation, decode weather patterns, and slice through clouds like a scene straight out of *Top Gun*. Let's be real, the bragging rights are worth it. "What did you do this weekend?" "Oh, just explored the skies over Seattle." Whether you choose to fly solo or team up with a buddy, you'll definitely rise above the ordinary. Websites like aopa.org can guide you on how to start, and local flight schools in your area offer hands-on training that'll have you flying into the sunset in no time. So, why wait? Take off and leave the ground behind because your adventure awaits in the wild blue yonder!

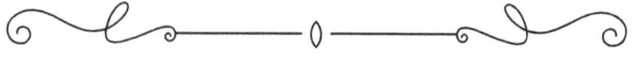

MASTER SWORD FIGHTING OR FENCING
Live Out Your Swashbuckling Dreams

Have you always secretly had a crush on pirate flicks or those epic medieval sword fights? Well, it's time to arm yourself (safely, of course) and dive into the thrilling world of sword fighting or fencing! This is more than a sport; it's a drama-filled escapade where you can feel like Zorro in real life. You can be at your local fencing club, channeling the elegance of a samurai or the swagger of a pirate. And hey, did I mention it's a fantastic workout? Say goodbye to your gym routine and hello to agility, balance, and a confident swagger that even Johnny Depp would envy. Maybe you're aiming for a trophy or just some killer bragging rights among friends? Sword fighting proves that the spirit of adventure, and a sprinkle of cheeky mischief is ageless. So un-sheath those stereotypes, because it's time to duel, and remember, even a sword fight won't save you from a bad online date. En garde!

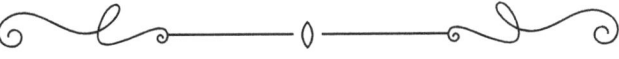

ENJOY RETIREMENT LIKE A QUEEN

Train as a Cirque du Soleil Performer

Learn Acrobatics, Aerial Silks, or Contortion

Cirque du Soleil isn't just for the young and sprightly; it's for anyone ready to defy gravity, even those who originally thought yoga was too much exercise. You can easily enroll in acrobatics or aerial silks classes at places like Circus Academy New York or AirFitNow and get ready to freak out your friends and maybe your chiropractor. Flip, spin, and climb your way into a new realm of flexibility and strength that'll leave everyone else in the dust. You may not run away with the circus, but you could definitely impress your family at the next holiday gathering when you casually mention, "Oh, me? I'm training to soar like a modern-day superhero." Say goodbye to the notion that aging means sitting on the couch with a cup of tea; instead, redefine it with a headstand and a cheeky wink. It's never too late to embrace your inner acrobat and make gravity your latest frenemy!

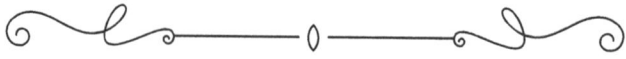

Volunteer at an Elephant Sanctuary in Thailand
Care for Gentle Giants

Swap out your usual routine for an unforgettable adventure and volunteer at an elephant sanctuary in Thailand! You could be spending your days feeding, bathing, and nurturing these majestic creatures while soaking in their incredible stories and supporting ethical tourism. It's a humbling and heartwarming experience that you won't forget, guaranteed! You'll also connect with fellow travelers from around the globe, bonding over your mutual adoration for these gentle giants. Whether you opt for a week-long trip or a couple of months, the memories you'll create are priceless, and don't even get me started on the stunning photos! Hello, future gallery wall. Retirement is the perfect opportunity to do something truly impactful. Why settle for another trinket from a souvenir shop when you can be part of something amazing? Websites like WWOOF (World Wide Opportunities on Organic Farms) or Volunteer World can help you find the perfect sanctuary. So, pack your bags, grab your sense of adventure, and get ready to change lives, starting with your own!

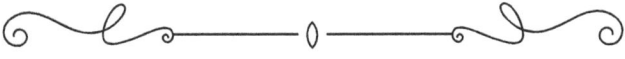

Change Up Your Look With a Bold Twist

Rock That Blue Streak

Ready to turn heads and own your fabulous self? Why not consider a daring blue streak, hot pink tips, or embracing your stunning silver strands? Changing your look is the ultimate "why not?" move. Hair is just hair until it's a statement piece. Go for that edgy cut from a local salon, try vibrant hues inspired by the latest TikTok trends, or flaunt your natural beauty with pride. A simple style switch can ignite confidence and catch attention, yes, those uninvited compliments might just flow! This isn't about "acting your age"; it's about being fearless, no matter if you're strutting through Target or sipping coffee at Starbucks. Hit up Pinterest for inspiration, then book an appointment with that stylist who's been setting Instagram on fire. Remember, it's all about owning your fabulous self, one bold strand at a time! So go ahead, make that change, and let the world see you shine like the star you are.

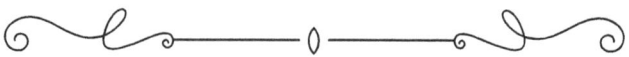

22

Use Social Media

Create a Podcast or YouTube Channel

Why should influencers have all the fun? Consider being adventurous and launching a podcast or YouTube channel and change the narrative on aging! Why not share your wild adventures, quirky hobbies, and hilarious opinions? Chat about whatever makes you tick. Talk about real life, debunk those myths, and show the world that retirement isn't a slow fade; it's a fab new beginning. Whether you're reviewing travel spots on TripAdvisor, trying extreme sports like bungee jumping (YouTube that!), or just cracking jokes about the chaos of daily life, your voice is valuable. Why not inspire other women to stop retiring in a small way? Retirement means being seen and heard, and what better way to do it than through your own platform? Use tools like Anchor for podcasts or Canva for creating eye-catching thumbnails. So, grab your smartphone, jot down some ideas, and remember, today's the day to shine! Lights, camera, action, it's your stage!

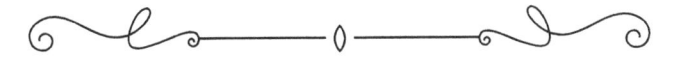

Love, Loss, and Elephants

Anne had always had a soft spot for animals. Even as a little girl, she was the one rescuing baby birds, sneaking neighborhood strays into the garage, and giving her stuffed animals their own bedtime routine. Volunteering at local shelters became a part of her DNA. But between work, raising three kids, and a husband who once called her "Dr. Doolittle with a mortgage," her time was always limited. Sunday mornings and the occasional holiday break were the best she could do.

Then retirement came, and so did the silence.

Her husband had passed three years earlier. Her kids were grown, chasing lives across different states. Anne found herself surrounded by a quiet house, an open calendar, and a question that kept tapping her on the shoulder: What now?

One evening, while scrolling through animal rescue stories, she stumbled upon something that stopped her cold: a three-month volunteer program at an elephant sanctuary in Chiang Mai, Thailand. Not a vacation. Not a photo-op. This was a get-your-hands-dirty, early-morning-feedings, mud-covered-boots kind of work.

Anne didn't hesitate.

Two months later, she arrived with a duffel bag, a wide-brimmed hat, and a heart ready for whatever came next. The sanctuary was breathtaking in the most grounding way with its lush, raw landscape and buzzing with life. There were no frills. Just rescued elephants healing from trauma, injury, and years of mistreatment.

Anne fed them, bathed them, and walked alongside them. She learned their names, their personalities, their favorite treats (any fruit). She cleaned up poop the size of boulders without flinching. She cried a lot—not from sadness, but from overwhelming awe. Every day, her heart cracked open a little more, not from grief, but from connection.

There was one elephant, Mae Suwan, who had lost her herd and arrived skittish and withdrawn. Over time, with patience and love, Anne earned her trust. On their final morning together, Mae Suwan gently wrapped her trunk around Anne's hand. It wasn't a goodbye, it was a thank you.

Anne took her only selfie that day. Dirt on her face, hair a mess, eyes full of tears and light.

For the first time in years, she didn't feel alone. She felt exactly where she was supposed to be—wildly, deeply alive.

The Wrap-Up: You're Just Getting Started

Who says retired women are supposed to play it safe? Not you! From chasing storms to flying planes, sword fighting, and ghost hunting, you've just proven that adventure has zero age limit. These ideas aren't just thrills; they're powerful reminders that you're still writing your bold, daring, and unapologetically fun story!

But hey, even the most fearless rebel needs her people. What's next? It's time to take that adventurous spirit out into the world and reconnect, mingle, and maybe even dance like everybody's watching. In the next chapter, we're diving into 11 ways to rule your social life in retirement because being social? That's a whole new adventure.

CHAPTER 3

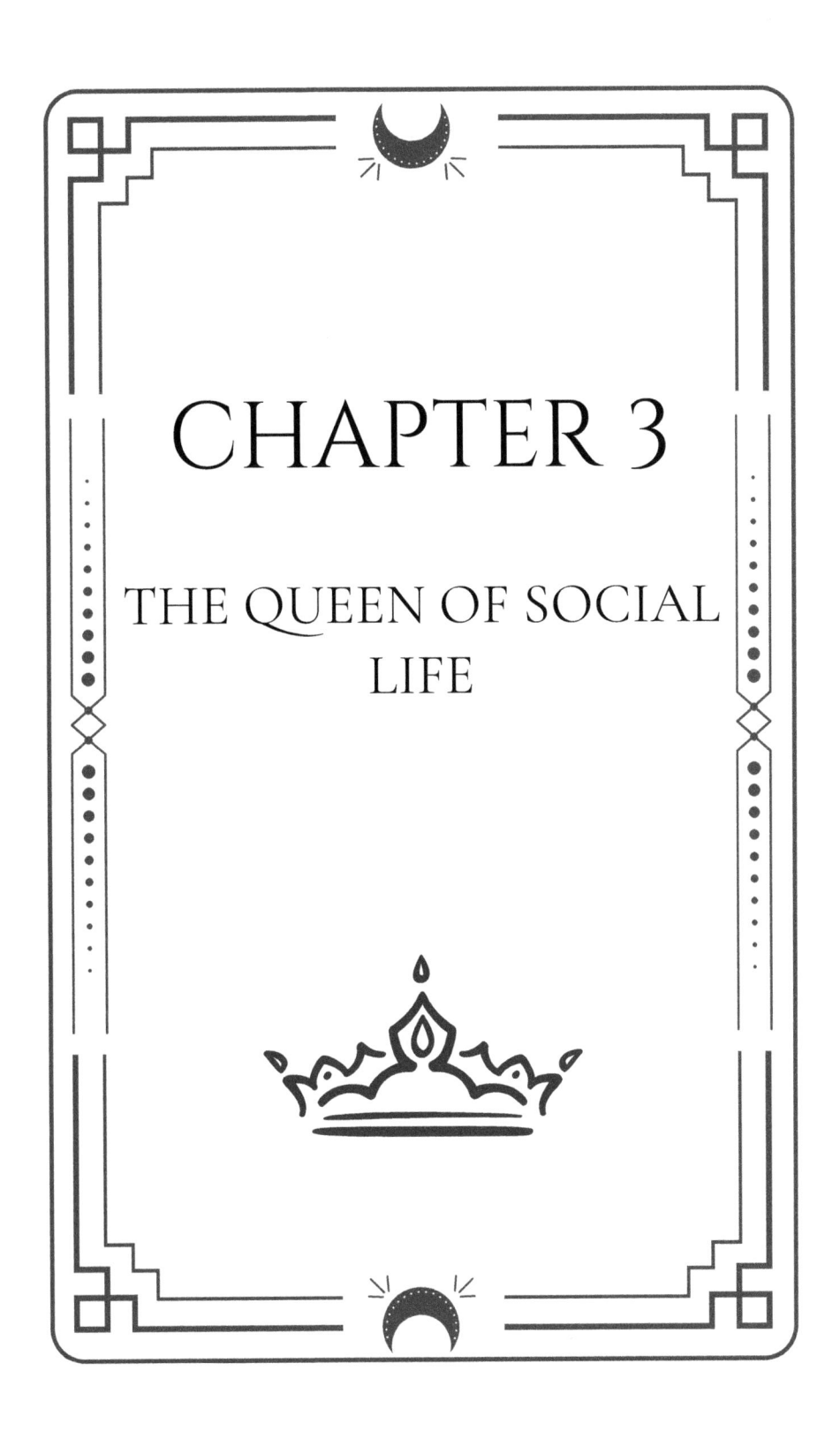

THE QUEEN OF SOCIAL LIFE

Retirement isn't your cue to shrink into the background, it's your chance to own the room, the park, the dance floor, or heck, even the local brewery. Forget small talk and stale coffee dates. This chapter is all about getting out there, making new connections, and turning every gathering into something worth talking about.

Whether you're meeting new friends, reconnecting with old ones, or charming complete strangers, these ideas will have you socializing in ways you never imagined. It's time to remember that your social life didn't retire and you're just getting started. Are you ready to mingle, laugh, and maybe stir up a little fun?

23

Host a Themed Dinner Celebrating Legendary Women

Are you ready to raise a glass to the trailblazers? Why not host a dinner party where each guest channels a legendary woman like Frida Kahlo, Eleanor Roosevelt, Beyoncé—whoever stirs your soul, really. Think themed menus that rival Instagram-worthy food trends from Taco Bell to the fanciest Michelin-starred joint, dramatic costumes, and conversations that spark all the feels. This is a fun, low-pressure way to learn new stories and celebrate the women who forged the paths we walk today and maybe remind everyone that you're becoming an icon, too. Wrap up the night with toasts, music playlists featuring empowering anthems from Spotify, and a few selfies that scream, "powerhouse vibes only." Because dinner is always richer when it's sprinkled with inspiration and let's be honest, a swipe of eyeliner that would make Cleopatra proud. So, order those themed decorations from your local party store and rally your friends through a group chat because it's time to celebrate the ladies who rock!

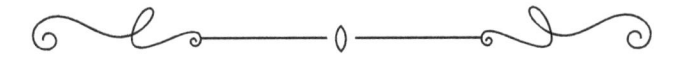

Attend Unconventional Events Like Speed-Friending or Mystery Dinners

It's time to forget awkward networking events and try speed-friending or a mystery dinner party instead! I want you to imagine social roulette where you toss small talk out the window and plunge into bizarre conversations with eager strangers. It's way more exciting than yet another book club meeting where everyone pretends to love the same novel. With speed-friending, you'll whizz through chats that reveal folks' quirks faster than you can say "Hello, my name is…" And mystery dinners? You waltz in, wonder who's at your table, and enjoy a meal that transforms into an adventure of taste and laughs. Want to dive into this? Check out websites like Meetup.com for local speed-friending events or stir up intrigue with DinnerParty.com's mystery dinner experiences. You never know who you might connect with, maybe a future best friend, or at least a hilarious tale to tell. So, lace up those social shoes, venture into the unknown, and rediscover life's delightful surprises!

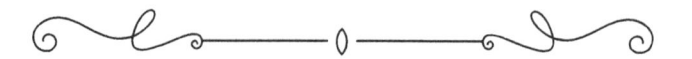

25

START AN EXCLUSIVE CLUB FOR SHARING WILD IDEAS

Why should kids have all the fun? Create an exclusive club where the main rule is: no boring conversations allowed. Meet monthly to share your wildest ideas, future adventures, or bucket list dreams. Want to open a llama rescue in the heart of Portland? Launch a rooftop garden like New York's Brooklyn Grange? Why not write a rom-com that tops Netflix charts? No idea is too big or too weird! It's part brainstorming session, part wine-fueled therapy, and truly, it's all about finding your tribe—those who aren't afraid to dream big with you. Imagine the shenanigans you could plan together! Then, after all that plotting, hit up websites like Meetup or Eventbrite to find inspiration for your next gathering. Remember, nothing bonds a group faster than scheming over coffee from your local café, cocktails at the nearest rooftop bar, or indulging in cupcakes from that bakery everyone's raving about. So gather your pals, unleash your imagination, and let's make the impossible possible, one quirky idea at a time!

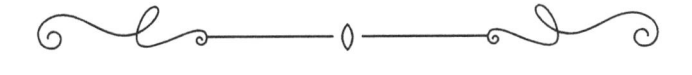

26

Take Part in an Escape Room Competition League

Put Your Problem-Solving to the Test

Gather your sharpest and sassiest pals and assemble the ultimate escape room dream team! Dive into the exciting world of local competitions where your group races against the clock and rival teams to tackle mind-bending puzzles and decode tricky clues. Try websites like Escape Room Directory to find venues near you! It's a delightful mix of cognitive acrobatics, heart-pounding thrills, and a hundred percent fun. Working together not only builds that electric "we crushed it!" vibe but turns mere acquaintances into lifelong buddies. Win or lose, you'll stroll out with an abundance of hilarious memories and more than enough reasons to hit up a nearby pub, like the local haunt on Yelp that has a killer happy hour. Who knew that flexing your brain could feel this entertaining? So, sharpen those sleuthing skills, gather your crew, and get ready for a whirlwind adventure that may or may not involve some friendly rivalries and a heap of laughter!

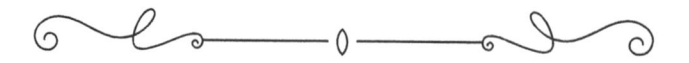

27

WRITE AND PERFORM A ONE-WOMAN SHOW

Get Up on That Stage!

Are you ready to step into the spotlight, literally? Why not write and perform your very own one-woman show? Are you brave enough to share your story, your wild escapades, your biggest heartbreaks, or the hilarious moments that deserve a real audience? Whether it's comedy, drama, or a quirky blend, owning the stage is a power trip! Check out local theaters, hit up open mic nights, or unleash your performance on YouTube. The world is your stage! You'll not only inspire others, but you'll also remind yourself that you're still the main character in your own epic tale. For inspiration, you can browse platforms like Eventbrite or Meetup to find fellow creators and live events. Engaging in something so personal is the kind of bold, audacious act that'll have you questioning why you didn't do it sooner. So grab your pen, channel your inner diva, and put on that dazzling performance. Take a bow because you've totally earned it!

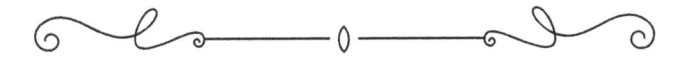

BE A STREET PERFORMER FOR A DAY

Experience the Thrill of Performing

Have you ever thought about grabbing a mic, strumming a guitar, or maybe unleashing a puppet on some unsuspecting pedestrians? Now's your chance! Spend a day as a street performer. Maybe you want to try singing, dancing, telling jokes, or reciting poetry? It's an exhilarating mix of nerve-wracking moments and pure thrill, plus an all-access pass to creativity. And let's be real, you'll walk away with anecdotes that'll steal the show at any dinner party. The icing on the cake? You might just sprinkle a bit of joy into someone's day and a few bucks for that espresso fix. Whether you're serenading the Statue of Liberty or cracking jokes in front of the Eiffel Tower, it's clear: Social connections can spark anywhere, even on a bustling sidewalk. Check out StreetPerformers.com or your local open mic night listing on Eventbrite for tips and to put ideas into action. Sometimes, you just have to take the plunge and make that sidewalk your very own stage!

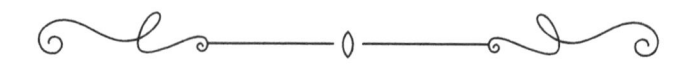

29

DESIGN A FASHION LINE FOR PEOPLE OVER 50

Reinvent Mature Style

Have you ever noticed that most "mature" fashion seems like it was dreamed up by someone who thinks fun is a dirty word? It's time to shake things up! Consider launching a fashion line that blares confidence, vibrant colors, and personality for those over 50 who refuse to blend into a sea of beige. Think edgy leather jackets from AllSaints, eye-catching prints like those from Desigual, or the kind of fierce glam you'd find at a New York City runway show. Create pieces that embody the fabulous phase you're in! Host a runway spectacle à la Project Runway, share your collection on Instagram, or throw a stylish gathering at your favorite brunch spot. Check out websites like Canva to design playful invites, or use Eventbrite to organize your soirée. No matter your approach, show the world that style, and life only gets brighter with age. Fashion isn't about dialing it down; it's about stepping out and shining bright, proving that every moment counts at any age!

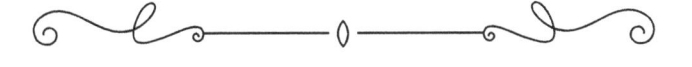

Be a Mentor for Young Female Entrepreneurs

Share Your Expertise

It's time to share your wisdom and become the Yoda of young female entrepreneurs! Whether it's tackling business plans like a seasoned pro or boosting confidence like a motivational TED Talk, your experience is pure gold. You could sign up for local initiatives through organizations like SCORE or participate in virtual mentorship communities on platforms like LinkedIn and Meetup. Better yet, establish your own group and call it "Boss Babes Unite" or something equally catchy. You'll be amazed at the electrifying energy that comes from guiding the next generation. Suddenly, you're not just offering advice; you're the superhero they didn't realize they needed. Plus, brace yourself because your mentees will turn out to be the best teachers too. After all, building a community is about lifting each other up like a well-timed high-five at a coffee shop in Seattle or a spontaneous dance party at the nearest entrepreneurial conference. Don't wait for the universe to align; dive in, share, and watch both you and your mentees soar!

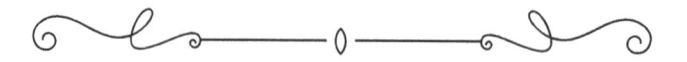

Host Wilderness Therapy Retreats
Help Others Reconnect With Nature

If the great outdoors makes you feel all warm and fuzzy inside, why not spread the joy? Organize wilderness therapy retreats where participants can unplug, breathe deeply, and have a heartfelt rendezvous with nature and themselves! Picture this: guided hikes through the stunning trails of the Appalachian Mountains, mindfulness sessions by the crystal-clear lakes of Tahoe, and fiery campfire chats reminiscent of summer nights at your favorite national park. You don't need a counseling degree, just a passion for the outdoors and the knack for creating a cozy, inviting atmosphere. Here's a fun twist: it's good for your soul, too! Nothing forges friendships quite like lying under the stars at Joshua Tree, sharing tales, and reminding ourselves that a little fresh air and maybe a s'more or two, is all we need. So grab your gear, rally the gang, and check out websites like Meetup or Eventbrite to get started. Who's ready to heal, laugh, and breathe in the wild? Count us in!

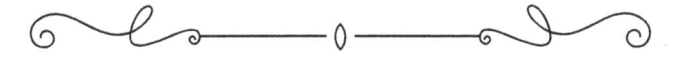

Take Up Roller Derby

Unleash Your Inner Rebel on Wheels

Ready to unleash your inner rebel? Lace up those skates and dive into the world of roller derby! It's fast, fierce, and yes, there might be a bruise or two, but trust me, it's empowering as hell. Roller derby is a sport as well as a full-on lifestyle all about building a tough, fearless community of like-minded skaters. You'll pick up new skills, get a solid workout, and maybe even snag a legendary nickname like "The Bulldozer" or "The Tornado." Plus, you'll meet fantastic women who know that life after 50 is about shifting into high gear, not slamming on the brakes. Whether you're blocking, jamming, or simply cruising like a boss at your local rink, this is one social scene where being tough is totally celebrated. So, gather your friends and check out resources like the Women's Flat Track Derby Association or local leagues on Meetup.com to roll into action!

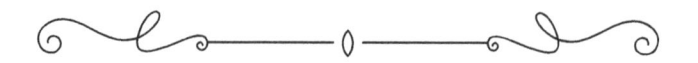

Host an Underground Supper Club

Exclusive, Themed Dining Experiences

Are you tired of the same old dinner parties? Idle chatter and boring food? It's time to spice things up with an underground supper club! I want you to imagine secret locations like a cozy speakeasy or a rooftop terrace. Think New York's "The Garret" vibes. Each gathering has a rotating theme, from Taco Tuesday to a Parisian bistro night that would make any foodie drool. Surprise menus keep your guests guessing and hungry for more! Whether you're in the kitchen channeling your inner chef or curating an experience worthy of a Michelin star, nothing beats a table full of friends, where every meal becomes an event. Want to crank up the fun? Add live music from a local artist you found on Bandcamp or storytelling that'll make everyone laugh until they cry and maybe even a fun dress code inspired by '80s movies! Food tastes even better when mixed with mystery, laughter, and the thrill of connection. Visit websites like Meetup or Eventbrite to find unique spaces to host your next culinary adventure!

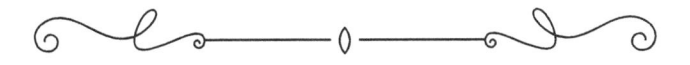

No Beige Allowed: Sharon's Fashion Rebellion

Sharon had always had a creative spark. She'd dabbled in painting, played with textiles, and even made her own prom dress back in 1976 complete with sequins and an illegal amount of tulle. But then life took over and she was raising kids, navigating meetings, juggling schedules, and the creative spark got tucked neatly behind PTA bake sales and a respectable 9-to-5.

A year into retirement, she finally had breathing room. And during one sunny afternoon coffee with friends, the conversation took a familiar turn: clothes.

"Everything looks like it was made for a teenager or my great-aunt Ethel," her friend Carol sighed, tugging at her overly bedazzled tunic.

"Why is everything either crop tops or cardigans with cats?" another chimed in.

Sharon laughed... but then paused. They were right. Their age group was being completely ignored by fashion. As if style had a shelf life, and she was done with being offered beige linen pants with stretchy waistbands as the pinnacle of wardrobe possibility.

That night, she pulled out her sketchbook.

She didn't want "sensible." She wanted bold, strong, beautiful. Clothes that moved well but didn't fade into the background. Sharon started sketching what she and her friends really wanted, sharp silhouettes, colors that popped, playful prints, breathable fabrics, and not a single elastic waistband in sight.

Within months, she'd created a mini collection and launched her brand: Second Act Style. Tagline? "We're retired, not invisible."

Her friends were her first models, sashaying through pop-up shows in cobalt jumpsuits and fierce wrap dresses. Strangers stopped them to ask, "Where did you get that?" and for the first time in a long time, the answer wasn't a sheepish "Oh, it's just something I found at the back of Target."

Sharon didn't just create clothes, she created a movement one pocketed jumpsuit at a time. No beige, and no apologies. Just strong, bold women dressing like they finally owned the room.

Because blending in was never really her style anyway.

The Wrap-Up: Your Social Reign Has Only Just Begun

Look at you stepping into the social spotlight like it was made for you. From themed dinners to roller derby and secret supper clubs, you're proving that life after retirement isn't about fading into the background, it's about making every moment an event. New friends, wild experiences, unforgettable nights—this is the social life you've earned, and it's only getting better.

Up next, revenge of the bucket list, where we tackle all those dreams you never had time for. Big, bold, maybe a little wild, and finally, all about you. Ready? Let's go check some boxes.

CHAPTER 4

REVENGE OF THE BUCKET LIST—DOING WHAT YOU NEVER HAD TIME TO DO

Retirement is no time to be riding off into the sunset. It's time to grab the reins, shouting "YEE-HAW!" and galloping straight toward the life you actually want. This chapter intends to show you how to get wonderfully wild, gloriously gutsy, and maybe even a little muddy. It's your time to tick off that bucket list, not with a dainty pencil, but with a glittery marker and some serious flair.

34

BECOME A TATTOO ARTIST SPECIALIZING IN FINE ART DESIGNS

If you've always had a flair for creativity, now is the perfect time to transform that passion into body art. Instead of confining your artistic talents to paper, consider becoming a tattoo artist who specializes in fine art designs. Look into apprenticeship opportunities at reputable tattoo studios, such as Ink Different Tattoo School, which offers programs tailored for aspiring artists of all ages. You could be mastering fine line work, crafting detailed botanical illustrations, and designing elegant portraits that will adorn the skin of your clients. Yes, queen, you are about to create walking masterpieces! This journey goes beyond merely etching designs for bikers; it represents a fresh chapter in your creative expression that embraces sophistication and uniqueness. Age is merely a number; you don't have to be in your 20s or experience a dark, brooding phase to thrive in the world of tattoo artistry. What you truly need are steady hands, bold confidence, and a willingness to learn. So, are you ready to dive into this vibrant world of ink and skin?

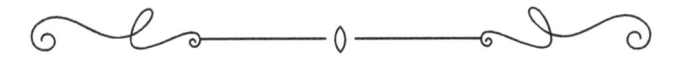

35

Travel to the North or South Pole

Forget the crowded cruises and the overpacked tourist traps that leave you feeling more like a number than a traveler. Imagine instead a remarkable adventure filled with penguins, colossal icebergs, and the unspoiled wild edges of our planet. Opt for a trip with companies like Quark Expeditions, where retirees are far from uncommon; in fact, they are celebrated. While you'll definitely want to pack your thermals for the chilly climates, what you'll receive in return are unforgettable stories that seem to freeze time. You could be raising a glass of glacial champagne in celebration of your retirement, surrounded by the majestic emperor penguins, their playful antics a delightful backdrop to your unique experience. Envision watching the midnight sun cast its golden glow over an untouched polar landscape, a privilege few can claim. So instead of lamenting over being "over the hill," it's time to welcome the idea that you're embarking on an exhilarating trek to the very tip of the Earth, ready to make memories that will last a lifetime.

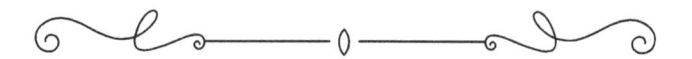

36

Move to a New Country for Three Months and Learn the Language from the Locals

Pack light, bring an open mind, and prepare for the ultimate glow-up because nothing says "I'm living my best retired life" like moving to a brand-new country and learning the local language from the people who actually speak it. Skip the boring textbooks and embrace café conversations, market haggling, and laughing your way through linguistic mix-ups that make life deliciously unpredictable. Programs like Workaway and Worldpackers offer unique opportunities to live abroad affordably while exchanging a few hours of help for room and board. Think helping out at a vineyard in France, an eco-lodge in Costa Rica, or a family-run farm in Italy. You'll not only learn the language, you'll become part of the community. Expect grandmas to correct your grammar mid-sentence and small kids to teach you slang your app never could. It's immersive, unforgettable, and totally empowering. Because you're not just visiting, you're living, laughing, and maybe even flirting… in a whole new language. Now that's retirement with some serious accent!

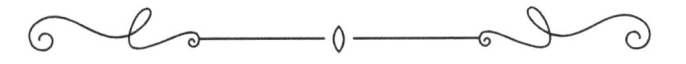

Become a Wedding or Elopement Officiant

You possess a unique wisdom and warmth that radiates far beyond what any ordinary justice of the peace can offer. Instead of settling for the mundane, you can easily become an officiant by getting ordained online through the Universal Life Church, a process that requires merely five minutes of your time with absolutely no cumbersome paperwork to figure out. Once you're ordained, the world becomes your oyster, allowing you to share your special talents on an international scale. Imagine officiating enchanting mountain-top elopements against the breathtaking backdrop of the Colorado Rockies, or conducting barefoot beach weddings on the sun-kissed shores of Tulum. There you are leading heartfelt ceremonies at the lush, romantic vineyards of Tuscany, celebrating love in its most beautiful and chaotic forms. This incredible opportunity lets you legally bless unions while embracing all the messy, magical moments that accompany love. And let's not forget one delightful perk, you often get to enjoy a slice of cake at the celebration! So, step into this wonderful role and start creating unforgettable memories.

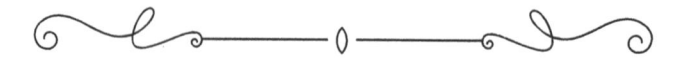

38

WORK ON A DUDE RANCH FOR A SEASON

Have you ever imagined waking up to the sight of majestic horses, with wide-open skies stretching endlessly above you and that faint, unmistakable scent of freedom in the air (yes, along with a hint of manure)? Companies like CoolWorks offer seasonal ranch jobs that attract a variety of adventurous spirits, with retirees often being the first to seize these incredible opportunities. Whether your role involves cooking delicious meals, guiding enthusiastic riders on unforgettable journeys, or simply soaking in those authentic cowboy vibes, this experience can be your very own Yellowstone moment, sans any of the drama. Can you envision yourself wrapped in a cozy flannel shirt, sipping coffee at the crack of dawn as the sun rises, and ending your day by falling asleep beneath a sparkling galaxy of stars? The cowboy lifestyle, with its rich traditions and carefree charm, feels surprisingly rewarding and fulfilling. Trust me, embracing the Yeehaw spirit truly looks *fantastic* on you, offering memories and experiences that will last a lifetime.

39

Be a Dog Sled Musher in Alaska

If you've ever found yourself excitedly shouting "Mush!" at your enthusiastic golden retriever, now may just be the perfect opportunity to channel that energy into something truly exhilarating. Dog sledding schools such as Alaska Dogstead and Wintergreen Dogsled Lodge located in Minnesota offer fantastic training for beginners eager to learn how to handle real sled dog teams. These incredible dogs are bred for speed and endurance, always ready to embark on an adventure and so are you. Imagine the sensation of the brisk wind whipping against your face as you race through the snowy landscapes, your heart pounding with excitement, reminding you that your adventurous spirit still thrives beneath all those cozy sweaters. It doesn't matter how many winters you've lived through; age is merely a number in the grand scheme of things. Dog sledding is truly more than just a sport; it's a lifestyle that beckons to those who seek adventure and a deeper connection with these remarkable canine companions. Embrace the thrill, and let the journey begin!

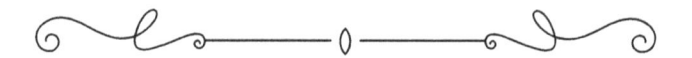

40

Live in an RV and Road Trip Through South America

Have you ever daydreamed about packing up your life into an RV and simply hitting the open road? There you are, on a path through South America, a continent brimming with breathtaking natural wonders. Imagine standing on the vast salt flats of Bolivia, where the landscape stretches endlessly under the bright blue sky, or feeling the mist on your face as you marvel at the majestic waterfalls of Argentina cascading down into lush valleys. To make your adventure even more enjoyable, you can join like-minded groups such as Overlander Oasis, or perhaps follow the insightful guides offered by PanAm Notes. If you want to be fully prepared, brush up on your Spanish language skills, which will enhance your experience as you park your cozy home on wheels in stunning locations, where llamas graze peacefully nearby. This journey focuses on reinventing yourself as you travel, exploring new horizons, and embracing life on the road. And don't worry, you can absolutely find Wi-Fi even in the remote beauty of Patagonia.

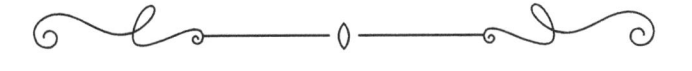

WRITE A CHOOSE-YOUR-OWN-ADVENTURE NOVEL

You've accumulated enough life experience to recognize that existence unfolds in a nonlinear fashion. So, why not craft a narrative that mirrors this complexity? Consider penning a novel in which the reader gets to make crucial decisions that influence the hero's journey. In this age of technology, tools like Twine empower you to construct interactive digital tales, giving readers the chance to immerse themselves deeply in the plot's twists and turns. Alternatively, if you prefer a more traditional approach, nothing beats the charm of putting pen to paper. Allow your boundless creativity to flourish: envision time-traveling detectives navigating the past, romantic space pirates embarking on thrilling escapades across galaxies, or perhaps a retired individual who adeptly unravels perplexing mysteries aboard lavish cruise ships. The ideas are limitless, and the stories you have within are just begging to be told. Let's venture together into a world where narratives are filled with unexpected turns, playful twists, and a hint of delightful scandal, creating an unforgettable reading experience.

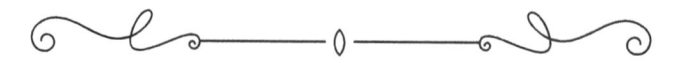

42

Run an Ultra-Marathon in the Desert

Sounds insane? That's precisely why it holds a coveted spot on your bucket list. Begin your adventure with a modest 5K if necessary. There are plenty of free and beginner-friendly apps available, like Couch to 5K, that can guide you every step of the way. Once you've built your confidence and endurance, set your sights on something truly extraordinary, such as the Marathon des Sables. This remarkable event involves a multiday run through the scorching heat of the Sahara desert. Will it be sweltering? Absolutely. Will you find yourself questioning your sanity? Undoubtedly. However, imagine the thrill of crossing that finish line, fully aware that you accomplished something that most people in their 30s wouldn't even contemplate. You'll emerge as a total badass, with blisters and battle scars that tell the story of your epic journey. Embrace the challenge, push your limits, and revel in the glory of having completed a feat of endurance that few dare to even dream of attempting. Your adventure awaits!

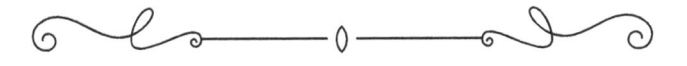

43

CLIMB AN ACTIVE VOLCANO

If life hasn't quite equipped you with a sense of power, consider the exhilarating experience of standing atop a smoking, rumbling mountain. Imagine the thrill as you conquer volcanoes like Mount Bromo in Indonesia, Pacaya in Guatemala, or perhaps the stunning Fagradalsfjall in Iceland. It's an adventure that promises to be both raw and risky, pushing you to embrace the elements in a truly unforgettable way. To embark on this journey responsibly, look for reputable tour operators such as G Adventures, which offer guided climbs ensuring both safety and a memorable experience. As you trek up these majestic giants, you'll be fully geared up, donning a sturdy helmet and wielding a walking stick, giving you an air of adventure that rivals even the most glamorous characters from fantasy tales, think a chic version of Gandalf. This isn't just about reaching a summit; it's about connecting with nature in its wildest form, feeling the heat from the ground, and witnessing the awe-inspiring power of Mother Earth in action.

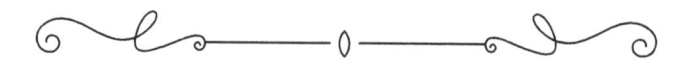

44

COMPETE IN A TOUGH MUDDER CHALLENGE

Crawling beneath barbed wire, leaping over roaring flames, and surfacing from the mud resembling a swamp goddess? Count us in! The Tough Mudder is not just a race; it's an ultimate test of camaraderie, joy, and pushing your boundaries to the limit. Gather your closest friends for training sessions, or form an adventurous squad of audacious retirees. It's time to kick off a group called "The Golden Mudders," how fun would that be?! Here's a pro tip: There's nothing that forges deeper connections among people quite like the shared experience of enduring mud from head to toe. As you conquer grueling obstacles and laugh through the mess, you'll create memories that last a lifetime. And once you cross that finish line, take the time to celebrate your achievements like the warriors you truly are. Raise a glass of wine, share hearty laughs, and indulge in the luxurious comfort of a long, relaxing bubble bath to wash away the dirt. It's all part of the Tough Mudder experience, uniting people while embracing the challenge head-on.

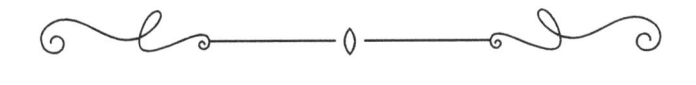

Hot Flash on a Volcano

Patti used to love hiking. Back in her 30s, she practically lived in her boots, scrambling up trails, chasing waterfalls, and pretending granola bars were a food group. But then life hit the gas pedal. Kids, carpooling, work deadlines, and eventually one cranky knee that demanded a replacement.

Her hiking boots got pushed to the back of the closet, buried behind PTA T-shirts and orthopedic sandals.

But one night, glass of wine in hand, watching a travel show about Guatemala, she saw it.

Pacaya. An active volcano. Smoky, dramatic, and so beautifully wild. Something deep inside her, maybe the same spark that used to sprint up switchbacks without Advil, lit up.

"I want to climb *that*," she said out loud.

Her best friend Linda raised an eyebrow. "You had a hard time climbing my porch last month."

But after a good laugh, they made a pact. Patti talked to her doctor, started walking daily, then added strength training, yoga, and a few four-letter words when her glutes protested. Linda kept her accountable, cheering her on and occasionally bribing her with coffee and trail mix.

Six months later, they flew to Guatemala, two retired women with strong knees, fierce hearts, and way too many wet wipes.

The climb wasn't easy. It was steep, hot, and smelled suspiciously like a burnt marshmallow. But with every step, Patti whispered, *I'm doing it.* And Linda echoed, *We're doing it.*

At the top, with lava crackling in the distance and sweat and tears dripping down their cheeks, they took *the* selfie. Arms wrapped around each other, faces beaming, utterly exhausted and completely alive.

No filter needed. Just pride, perseverance... and a little volcanic sass.

The Wrap-Up: Bucket List? Consider It Stomped in Heels

So, let's get one thing straight: Retirement is the sparkly second act where you finally stop asking permission and start living out loud. You've got wisdom, wild dreams, and a whole lot of time to stir up the kind of fun that would make your 25-year-old self jealous. Whether you're inking art, running through deserts, or officiating weddings on cliffs, this is your revenge era, and the bucket list doesn't stand a chance.

And if you're still worried you're "too old" or that retirement means slowing down? Honey. Please. Turn the page. Because next up, we blow up every outdated stereotype and build a bold, brilliant new image of what it really means to be retired and radiant. You're not fading, you're just warming up.

CHAPTER 5

I'M NOT DEAD, I'M JUST GETTING STARTED—REDEFINING WHAT RETIREMENT LOOKS LIKE

ENJOY RETIREMENT LIKE A QUEEN

Retirement is not a soft fade into beige cardigans and birdwatching... It's a reawakening. A revolution. A raucous declaration that you are just getting started, and the world better keep up. This chapter flips the outdated script about aging women and replaces it with rhinestones, glitter, mischief, and power poses.

45

Be an Extra in a TV Show or Movie

Have you ever dreamed of briskly trailing behind someone in a tense hospital scene or pretending to savor a cup of coffee during a heartfelt monologue in a romantic comedy? Now is your opportunity to embrace being delightfully unnoticeable right in front of the camera. Being a background extra is not only absurdly enjoyable but also surprisingly empowering. Websites such as Casting Networks or Central Casting frequently seek real individuals of all ages and diverse backgrounds for various shows, films, and commercials. No acting experience is necessary; what's required is simply a bit of patience and the ability to appear engaged while pretending to sip from an imaginary coffee cup. Imagine the joy on your family's faces when they catch a glimpse of you in the background of a show like Law & Order: Retired & Fabulous. Even if your close-up ends up being blurry and fleeting, it's still a moment to cherish. Extra points if you let out a dramatic gasp during a scene and the director decides to keep it! Instead of disappearing, you're infusing a touch of flair into the vibrancy of the entertainment industry, queen.

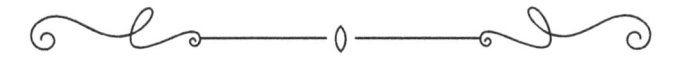

46

Get a Dramatic Haircut or Color for No Reason at All

You've adhered to enough guidelines in life, always sticking to what's deemed "age-appropriate." Now, as you prepare for your next brunch gathering, it's the moment to step outside that box and flaunt your turquoise curls or a daring mohawk. No explanations should be needed, just a simple, "I felt like it." Your hair serves as one of the most exhilarating avenues to reclaim your sense of individuality, and the moment you make that change, you'll feel the transformation resonate within you. The surge of confidence? Absolutely electric. The astonished reactions from those around you? Utterly scrumptious. And the sense of liberation? Truly unparalleled. Seek out a stylist who thrives on bold transformations, as they live for requests just like yours. Alternatively, stroll into an edgy salon featuring vibrant neon lights and simply say, "Surprise me." If you're not quite ready to take the plunge with a radical change, start small with peekaboo pink streaks or try out a fauxhawk. Remember, transformative hair doesn't signify a midlife crisis; it subtly whispers midlife magic. When the cashier at Trader Joe's admires your hair and exclaims, "Wow, love the hair," you'll be able to smile and reply, "Thanks! I've just embraced my inner rockstar."

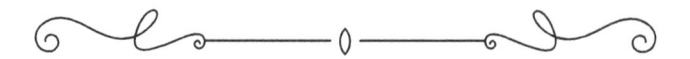

47

Start a Band, Even If You Don't Play an Instrument

Call It the Menopause Mavericks and Fake It Till You Make It

Yes, you! It doesn't matter if the last instance you graced the stage was at your child's kindergarten concert, or if you've never strummed a guitar before. Starting a band in retirement is less about chasing after Billboard chart success and much more about embracing the joy, laughter, and delightful chaos that comes from creating music with friends. Gather a fearless ensemble of like-minded companions and craft a sound that's entirely yours, perhaps a blend of "garage glam" with a twist of "grannycore disco fusion." There are no limitations; let your imagination run wild! Utilize apps like GarageBand to simulate your way into musical brilliance or discover online tutorials on YouTube that can guide you as you master the art of playing a triangle solo. And if all else fails, feel free to express yourself by banging on a tambourine while belting out uplifting lyrics such as, "I survived menopause and I'm still fabulous!" Local open mic events and community centers offer ideal venues for your debut. Remember, you're not aiming for fame; you're here to completely unleash your creativity. Even if you don't become an overnight sensation, you'll undoubtedly leave a legendary mark!

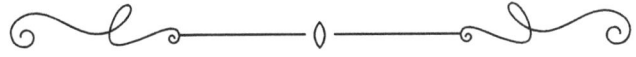

48

Go to a Tattoo Parlor and Let the Artist Pick for You

This one is not for the faint of heart but it is very on-brand for anyone redefining what it means to be retired. Walk into a trusted tattoo studio, maybe one you've stalked on Instagram for months, and give the artist one magical instruction: "Surprise me." Will you end up with a delicate flower? A lightning bolt? Maybe a tiny alien drinking coffee? Who knows and that's the fun. This spontaneous act is about surrendering control and celebrating unpredictability. It's about trusting your gut and saying yes to something a little wild. Want a safety net? Give the artist a theme like "nature" or "magic" and let them create within that vibe. Sites like Inkbox even let you try temporary tattoos in case you want to dip a toe before diving into permanent ink. Either way, this is a bold rebellion against the idea that women over 60 have to play it safe. You're not playing anything safe, you're living loudly.

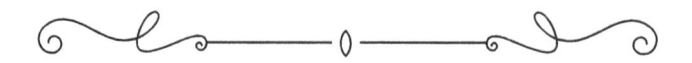

49

Do a Professional Photoshoot with a Wild Theme

Forget about the stiff family portraits and those pastel cardigans that do little to express your true self. This is the perfect opportunity to unleash your inner diva, warrior, or even a time-traveling pirate queen, serving looks that could absolutely melt a camera lens. Seek out a photographer who understands and embraces your vision. Better yet, consider collaborating with a talented local makeup artist and stylist who can fully immerse you in a world of fantasy. Want to don golden armor while frolicking in a vibrant field of wildflowers? Absolutely yes! Craving a dramatic smoky eye paired with a dazzling sequin jumpsuit, all beneath a shimmering disco ball? Even better! Websites such as Thumbtack and The Bash can connect you with creative professionals right in your area. Aim to capture that perfect shot, and don't forget to share it online. Make it your next Christmas card or, better yet, your ultimate legacy. This experience is all about capturing your power, joy, and outrageous sense of fun. Long after the photo shoot is over, those stunning images will serve as constant reminders that you're not simply growing old; you're growing iconic.

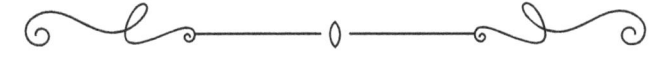

50

Throw a "Roast Me" Party Where Friends Make Fun of You (With Love, Of Course!)

If you can't laugh at yourself in retirement... when can you? A "Roast Me" party is your chance to gather your closest, sassiest friends and invite them to lovingly mock your quirks, bad habits, and that time you tried to become a minimalist and bought 19 baskets from HomeGoods "to get organized." Think of it like a birthday party, but instead of gifts, you get jokes. And instead of candles, there's wine. Lots of wine. Set the tone by roasting yourself first—maybe read your teenage diary out loud or share your most dramatic Amazon purchase history. Make it playful, not mean. For example, nobody gets to bring up your ex-husband unless it's really, really funny. You'll be surprised how liberating it is to laugh at your own legend. After all, self-deprecating humor is the ultimate power move. Plus, it gives everyone permission to be real, raw, and ridiculously funny. There are bonus points if it's recorded for future blackmail.

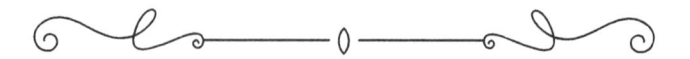

51

Go to an Open House of a Mansion You Can't Afford and Pretend You're a Billionaire

Some people go to open houses to find their dream home. You, however, are going to channel your inner Real Housewife billionaire energy and treat this like a full-on performance. Put on your biggest sunglasses, grab a friend as your "assistant," and waltz into that multimillion-dollar mansion like you're scouting your third summer property. Ask questions like, "Do the marble floors clash with caviar spills?" or "Is the wine cellar secure enough for my royal collection?" Drop wild, fake hints with a straight face: "We'll have to ship the giraffes separately, the last time was such a hassle." Realtors may smile nervously, but trust me, they've seen worse. And who knows? You might actually find décor ideas, or better yet, a new role as a mystery heiress with an outrageous backstory. You're not dreaming small anymore. You're trying on lives for fun. And in all honesty, you're the kind of woman who makes a mansion feel lucky you showed up.

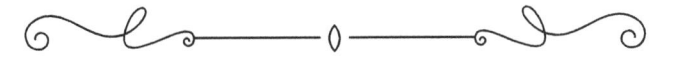

52

Create a Social Media Persona That's Completely Outrageous

Bored of the same old travel photos and cat memes? It's time to shake up the algorithm with a whole new online identity. Create a social media account under an alter ego like Countess Sapphire, Gloria Goldspark, or Lady Lavish of Palm Springs. Post glam selfies, absurd advice, fake "sponsored" products like diamond-encrusted slippers or psychic tea, and throw in the occasional mysterious caption: "The yacht leaves at dawn. Only bring secrets." Your friends won't know what's real, your grandkids will be confused and impressed, and you'll rediscover just how much fun it is to be completely unpredictable. Use apps like Canva or CapCut to design stories and videos that are so fabulous they're borderline performance art. Is it silly? Yes. Is it the best thing you'll do all month? Also yes. Social media isn't just for 20-somethings doing dances in parking lots, it's for retired queens rewriting the internet one glittery post at a time.

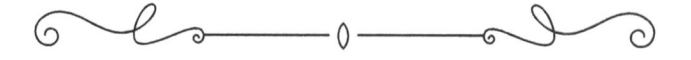

Attend a Live Auction and Make a Fake Bid Just to Feel the Power

There's something oddly thrilling about raising a paddle at a live auction. It's the perfect mix of danger, drama, and rich-people cosplay. Whether it's an art auction, charity gala, or antique bidding war, show up in something dramatic (a big hat helps) and sit near the front. Even if you don't actually plan on buying anything, just act like you might. When the bidding starts, casually lift your paddle. Then lower it and shake your head as if the art just isn't quite museum-worthy enough. Whisper to your neighbor, "I already have two of those." You don't need to buy anything. The thrill is in the pretending. But fair warning: If your paddle goes up at the wrong moment, you may end up the proud owner of a vintage canoe or an abstract sculpture that looks like spaghetti. Still worth it? Absolutely. Nothing screams I'm not dead, I'm just dramatic like bidding on an oil painting called Sadness in Velvet.

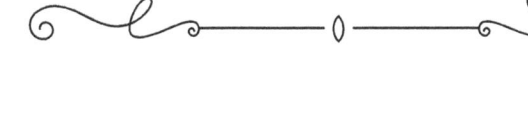

54

Plan a Road Trip With Absolutely No Destination in Mind

This isn't your standard, meticulously organized itinerary complete with scheduled bathroom breaks and carefully packed emergency snacks. No, this is chaos road-tripping, retirement edition. All you truly need for this adventure is a full tank of gas, a playlist packed with empowering bangers that get your spirit soaring, a trusted friend or perhaps your favorite solo travel alter ego, and of course, a coin. At every significant intersection or decision point, simply flip the coin. If it lands on heads, veer left; if it's tails, veer right. Your journey might lead you to a charming roadside diner where the pancakes are decadently delicious, or perhaps to a quaint town so tiny that its gas station doubles as a bait shop and hosts a lively karaoke night. Expect to get lost, take unexpected photos that capture the essence of spontaneity, and you might even stumble upon the best slice of pie in a locale that doesn't even register on Google Maps. The beauty of this adventure is that you are not just a passenger; you are the ride itself. After years spent adhering to maps, timetables, and societal expectations, now is your time to chase your whims, and maybe a quarter.

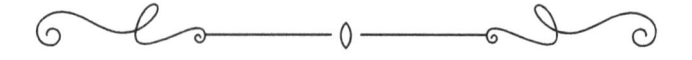

55

Sign Up for a Local Theater Play with Zero Acting Experience

You don't need any formal training. You don't need a resume filled with stage experience. What you truly need is the courage to step into your local community theater audition and proclaim, "I'm ready to try something different." It doesn't matter if you land a leading role or find yourself as "Confused Townsperson #4"; every experience is a treasure. The world of theater isn't measured by perfection, it's all about your presence. You'll encounter a wonderfully eccentric group of fellow misfits who will welcome you with open arms and laughter. Before you know it, you'll be sharing countless giggles during rehearsals, stumbling over lines, and who knows, you might even unearth a surprising knack for delivering dramatic death scenes! Many local theater groups are excited to embrace spirited retirees, and productions like *Mamma Mia!* or *The Importance of Being Earnest* practically plead for your unique flair. So, don your costume, don the wig, and belt out those tunes with gusto. Forget "aging gracefully"—you're embracing life loudly, complete with jazz hands and all!

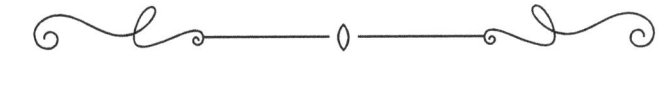

56

Hire a Chauffeur for a Day and Insist on Being Called "Madam"

Life is indeed fleeting, and everyone deserves a day to embrace their inner slightly unhinged heiress. Imagine booking a local car service or opting for a luxurious platform like Blacklane. Dress to impress in a style that fuses old money sophistication with the quirky charm of an eccentric aunt. Spend the day cruising through town with an air of royalty; order a refreshing mocktail or a chilled glass of champagne, and effortlessly slip on a pair of oversized sunglasses while avoiding any door handles. As you glide through the city, don't shy away from making whimsical requests to your driver, such as, "Please take the scenic route; I need to clear my busy mind," or "Let's make a detour to the art gallery; I feel like adopting a Monet today." If anyone dares to inquire about your identity, respond with a nonchalant, breathy, "Just someone who's finally found the time to truly savor life." Embrace this delightful fantasy; you've earned it! It's not merely about extravagance but rather joyfully amplifying the essence of who you already are. And if a stranger snaps a photo of you from across the street, mistaking you for a famous personality, well, perhaps you are!

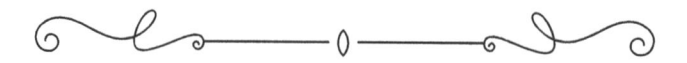

The Spotlight Called and She Answered

Six months into retirement, Diane realized something was missing. It wasn't money, or sleep, or freedom—she had plenty of that now. It was something older. Something she'd buried way back in high school behind geometry homework and awkward prom photos.

She wanted to be on stage.

She used to dream of it, stealing the spotlight in school plays, belting out solos, becoming someone else for just a little while. But then, well... life. Diapers needed changing. Clients needed charming. Her husband needed her, her kids needed everything, and she shelved that dream somewhere between PTA meetings and quarterly reports.

But now? Now it was her time.

On a chilly Tuesday evening, she walked through the glass doors of her local community theater. It was try-out night for a small-town comedy. Diane had no acting credits, no monologue prepared, and no idea what she was doing. But she stood on that stage, heart pounding, and said, "Hi. I'm Diane. I've always wanted to do this."

She landed a part.

Not just any part but a sassy supporting role with real lines, real laughs, and real costume changes. That night at dinner, she declared, "For the next eight weeks, I'll be at rehearsal every night. Just so you know."

Her husband blinked, fork midair, and then smiled.

Opening night came with shaky knees and a stomach full of butterflies. But when those stage lights came on, Diane lit up. Her family, kids, grandkids, husband, sister, and neighbors took up an entire row, clapping like wild and wiping away tears.

Because there she was. Not just retired, not just "Mom" or "Nana" or "Honey."

She was Diane. Fearless, radiant, hilarious, alive, and absolutely glowing under the lights of a dream reignited.

The Wrap-Up: Long Live the Queen Energy

If you've made it this far and you're still worried about retiring the way you are "expected" to," it's time we officially retire that phrase from your vocabulary, along with "sensible shoes" and "I shouldn't." You're not retiring into invisibility. You're moving into main character energy. This chapter of life doesn't center around rebellion, it's all about reminding you that reinvention doesn't have an expiration date.

You're not winding down. You're just getting warmed up. You've got flair, grit, glitter, and a glorious sense of humor and now, the world gets to see it all, unfiltered.

And sure, you've shaken up the outside world with dramatic hair, fake mansion bids, and alter egos but what about your inner world? What happens when you want to spend your days doing something meaningful, creative, and most importantly, not mind-numbingly dull?

Turn the page, because next up is hobbies that won't bore you to death, where crochet is just the beginning and boredom is officially banned. Let's find out what lights your fire.

CHAPTER 6

HOBBIES THAT WON'T BORE YOU TO DEATH (LITERALLY)

I get it, if one more person suggests you take up lawn bowling or start a "nice little book club," you might start throwing things. Look, no shade to cozy hobbies (you do you, scarf queens), but if your soul craves something with a bit more zing, you're in the right chapter.

Retirement isn't your cue to quietly collect stamps and wait for dinner at 4:30. It's your time to finally say, "I've always wanted to try that… and now I will."

This chapter is for the bold, the curious, the slightly unhinged (in the best way), and anyone who believes life's second act should be more thrilling than your first. Whether you're learning sword fighting, starting a YouTube channel, or becoming a certified cheese sculptor (yes, it's a thing), we're ditching the dull and diving headfirst into the unexpected.

Warning: You might laugh, get dirty, or accidentally become really good at something bizarre. Let's find a hobby that makes you feel alive, not just "occupied."

57

Urban Beekeeping

Have Your Own Honey Empire Without Leaving the City

Move over, suburban backyard gardeners, there's a new queen in town, and she's wearing a beekeeping suit. Urban beekeeping is buzzing (pun intended), and it's perfect for anyone who wants a sweet hobby that's good for the planet and ridiculously satisfying. You don't need a full farm, just a rooftop, balcony, or tiny garden space and a lot of curiosity. Programs like Best Bees or local cooperative groups will help you get started without getting stung, literally or financially. You'll learn how to care for your hives, protect the bee population, and harvest your own honey. Picture it: jars of "Queen B's Golden Glow" on your kitchen shelf, or better yet, sold at your local farmer's market. Friends will line up for your lavender-infused batch. It's also shockingly meditative, watching bees work their magic has been known to lower stress. Just don't name them all. They're not pets… no matter how much you start talking to them.

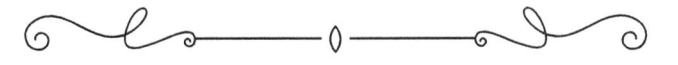

58

TRAIN AS A CHOCOLATIER AND LAUNCH A BOUTIQUE BRAND

You've always loved chocolate (who hasn't?), but now it's time to go from connoisseur to *creator*. Becoming a chocolatier isn't just a delicious dream, it's a sweet, sensory-filled journey into the world of glossy ganache and perfectly tempered truffles. Enroll in workshops through programs like Ecole Chocolat, or take hands-on local classes that teach everything from cocoa sourcing to flavor balancing. Once you've got the basics, the possibilities are endless. Want to make spicy mango chili bark or dark chocolate bourbon caramels with sea salt? Do it. Better yet, give your brand a cheeky name like *Hot Flash Fudge* or *Not Your Daughter's Chocolate*. Package them beautifully and sell them at markets or online. Every batch you create will not only taste amazing, it'll remind you that it's never too late to master something deliciously decadent. Chocolate is a language of love, indulgence, and artistry... and now, it's your newest way to shine.

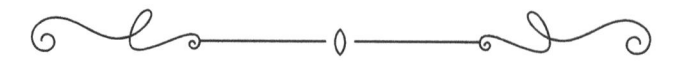

59

Becoming a Fire Dancer
Light Up the Night With Pyrotechnic Performance Skills

Yes, you read that right. Fire dancing, and yes, with real actual flames. Did I mention they are on sticks and spinning? And before you panic, no, you don't have to set yourself on fire. That's not the goal. That's called a mistake. Fire dancing is a mesmerizing mix of movement, rhythm, and total badassery. You can train with tools like poi, staff, or hula hoops, starting with non-flaming versions before you graduate to the real deal. Local circus schools, flow arts communities, or even retreats like Ignite Retreat can help you master the art. You'll work your core, boost your coordination, and command attention like a sparkly flame goddess at your next backyard party. And how cool would it be telling someone at a dinner party? "Oh me? I fire dance now," is the ultimate mic drop. It's thrilling. It's empowering. It's the definition of lit, in every sense. Just make sure your fire extinguisher is nearby and your eyebrows are accounted for.

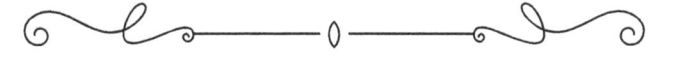

60

Laughter Yoga

Burn Calories and Brighten Moods

Let me ask you a question. Have you tried yoga? Okay, now have you tried group fitness? Wonderful. Now, have you ever giggled your way through a full workout? Laughter yoga combines intentional laughter with yogic breathing, and yes, it feels weird at first. But then something beautiful happens: your fake giggles become real cackles. You bond with strangers. Your abs hurt. And suddenly, your mood skyrockets. Founded by Dr. Madan Kataria, this practice has gone global, with laughter clubs popping up everywhere (Cann, 2021). It's free, joyful, and surprisingly cathartic. You'll be clapping, ho-ho-ha-ha-ing, and doing goofy movements that lower stress hormones, boost endorphins, and make you feel like a kid on a sugar high. No flexibility or Lycra required, just a willingness to look ridiculous in public. Which you've earned the right to do. In a world full of seriousness, laughter yoga is your new rebellion. Go ahead, laugh like your happiness depends on it because… it kind of does.

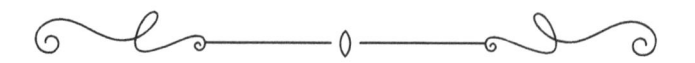

61

COMPETITIVE AXE THROWING

It's Surprisingly Therapeutic

There's something wildly satisfying about hurling a sharp object at a wooden target while people cheer you on. Competitive axe throwing is the sport you didn't know you needed in your life, but once you try it, you'll wonder how you ever managed stress without it. It's the perfect combo of focus, physical release, and bragging rights. Axe bars and leagues are popping up in cities everywhere (check out WATL to find a spot near you), and yes, they welcome beginners. You'll be shocked at how quickly you go from awkward flinger to confident blade-slinger. And let's be honest: it's better than screaming into a pillow. Plus, you'll meet a wild little community of people who also like throwing sharp things… for fun. Whether you're working through grief, rage, or just general Tuesday-level tension, axe throwing says, "I'm strong, I'm fierce, and I don't need elastic waistbands to prove it." Aim high. Swing big. And hit bullseyes, in life and in lumber.

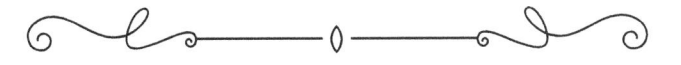

62

ARTICIPATE IN AN INTERNATIONAL REALITY SHOW

Travel and Compete in Something Wild

Are you tired of watching *The Amazing Race* and yelling, "I could do that!" at the screen? Well, now it's time to prove it. From travel competitions to quirky international game shows, there's a world of reality TV looking for fabulous, fearless personalities of every age, just like you. You can check casting sites like Backstage, or even international platforms where you can apply for travel challenges, cooking competitions, or outlandish social experiments that hopefully don't involve eating bugs, but no promises. Whether you're racing across Morocco or attempting a pottery throwdown in Portugal, these shows love a good underdog story, and who's more compelling than a retired woman with grit, charm, and zero tolerance for drama? You'll travel, meet wild characters, and do things you never imagined, on camera. You'll get bonus points when your grandkids lose their minds when you show up on Netflix. Retirement glow-up? More like retirement takeover. Get ready for your close-up.

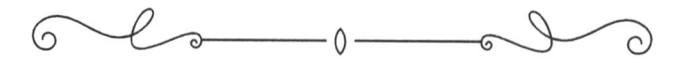

63

Take Part in an Escape Room Competition League

Put Your Problem-Solving to the Test

Forget Sudoku and crossword puzzles, *this* is the brain-boosting thrill you didn't know you needed. Escape rooms are no longer just a fun Friday night activity—they've become full-on competitive sports, complete with leagues, tournaments, and bragging rights. These games throw you into thrilling, themed adventures where you solve puzzles, crack codes, and yell "I found the key!" more than you ever thought possible. Find a local escape room that hosts team nights or join a group through Escape Room League or Meetup. No experience needed, just a curious mind, a love for mystery, and maybe reading glasses for the fine print. You'll boost your memory, fire up your logic skills, and laugh like crazy when your group accidentally traps itself in the fake morgue room (true story). The best part? It's active, social, and satisfying. And when you finally break out with five seconds left on the clock? Victory tastes so much sweeter than bingo.

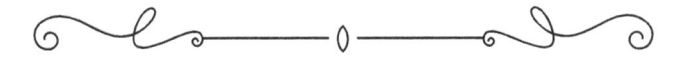

64

DIY Taxidermy With a Twist
If You've Ever Wanted to Bedazzle a Squirrel... Now's Your Chance

Before you ask, yes, this is real. And no, it's not nearly as creepy as you think. Well, okay, maybe it is a little creepy, but also strangely delightful. Modern taxidermy is making a comeback, especially the artsy, tongue-in-cheek kind. Think punk-rock raccoons in tiny leather jackets or a squirrel wearing rhinestone sunglasses and holding a disco ball. Workshops like those hosted by Divya Anantharaman or quirky art studios teach ethical, sustainable taxidermy using animals that were already deceased. The best part? You are not required to go squirrel hunting. All you need to do is add glitter, tiny hats, or fairy wings, and yes, you can even make a woodland drag queen. It's equal parts art, biology, and plenty of wicked humor. Your creation will either shock your guests or become the weird centerpiece of your living room, and both are wins. No, this is not your typical retirement craft, but you're not exactly a typical retiree, right?

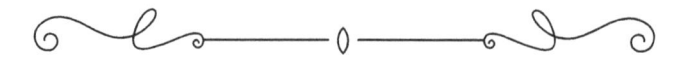

Ghost Hunting

Prove Once and for All Whether Aunt Martha's House Was Actually Haunted

Who you gonna call? You, apparently. Ghost hunting is no longer reserved for edgy YouTubers and people with questionable EMF meters. It's become a fascinating, techy, and often hilarious way to explore haunted places and test the limits of what you believe. Why not join a ghost tour or local paranormal investigation group? They're everywhere. You can try Ghost Hunt Weekends or regional meetups. Grab a friend or two and learn how to use spirit boxes, thermal cameras, and good old-fashioned goosebumps. Why not visit historic prisons, abandoned hospitals, or haunted inns, and don't forget snacks and a flashlight? Whether or not you find a ghost, you will find scares, fascinating stories, and late-night laughter. And if you do happen to record a spooky voice saying your name? Just calmly say, "Not today, spectral friend," and carry on with your fabulous life. You're not afraid of aging, and you're definitely not afraid of ghosts.

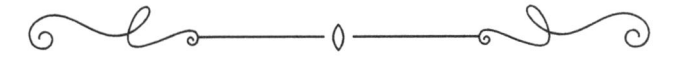

66

BE A MYSTERY SHOPPER FOR HIGH-END BRANDS

Get Paid to Shop and Review

Do you adore shopping? Do you have a knack for judging everything from product packaging to customer interactions? If so, mystery shopping could be the perfect retirement gig for you! This isn't just any ordinary task—mystery shopping has evolved into a luxurious endeavor. High-end brands are searching for discerning shoppers to evaluate customer service, product quality, and overall posh experiences. You can join reputable platforms like Market Force, IntelliShop, or Secret Shopper to get started. They'll assign you to various establishments. Think upscale stores, gourmet restaurants, luxurious spas, and even fancy car dealerships. Your job? Simply immerse yourself in the shopping experience, jot down your observations, and report back. The cherry on top? Some assignments allow you to keep the items you buy. A designer lipstick from Chanel? Yes, please! Or perhaps a lavish massage at that posh spa you've been eyeing? It's all for the sake of market research, after all. You'll feel like a chic undercover agent, blending elegance with judgment and a unique opportunity to critique, all while enjoying fabulous perks.

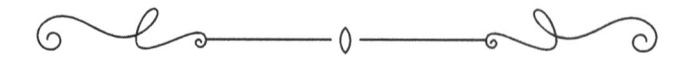

67

Follow the Migration Path of Monarch Butterflies

Travel With Nature

Monarch butterflies journey over 3,000 miles annually, graceful, winged explorers navigating by instinct and sunlight. Does that resonate? If your spirit craves beauty and meaning, this hobby is nothing short of enchanting. You can literally accompany the butterflies on their migration, commencing in Canada or the US and venturing all the way to the enchanting forests of Michoacán, Mexico, where millions of these monarchs congregate each winter. Programs like the Monarch Joint Venture and guided eco-tours allow you to witness their magnificent migration firsthand, while also supporting vital conservation efforts. You'll embark on hikes, gain knowledge, bond with fellow nature enthusiasts, and perhaps shed a tear when you first witness the sky filled with vibrant orange wings. There's a profound spirituality in pursuing beauty across borders. Remember, retirement isn't about stagnation; it's about moving with purpose. So, why not become part of this extraordinary journey? Embrace the call of the butterflies, and allow their migration to inspire your own meaningful adventures!

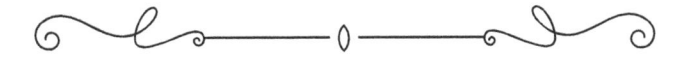

68

Professional Baby Cuddler
Uh Huh, It's Real

You've rocked babies to sleep. You've held little heads with love. And now? You can put those gentle arms to real use again, as a professional baby cuddler. Many hospitals have NICUs where newborns, often born prematurely or going through withdrawal, need the comfort of a human touch, but their parents aren't always able to be there. That's where you come in. Hospitals around the country run cuddle care programs, and volunteers are trained to hold, soothe, and snuggle these tiny warriors. No, you don't have to change diapers. No, you don't have to stay overnight. But yes, you will likely tear up daily as you feel those tiny hands wrap around your finger. It's more than a feel-good hobby. Studies show cuddling improves infant health outcomes, regulates heart rates, and reduces pain responses (Yoshida & Funato, 2021). You won't just be passing time, you'll be giving love in its purest form. And honestly? There's no sweeter way to spend a Tuesday afternoon.

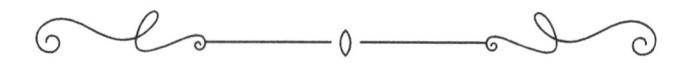

Wings of Her Own and Zero Regrets

Margaret had spent 38 years in scrubs. Not the cute kind from TV dramas, but the practical, pocket-stuffed kind that smelled like antiseptic and mystery bodily fluids. She was a nurse, a mother of three, a life wrangler, a crisis manager, and an occasional bedtime therapist. Retirement was supposed to feel like a parade of peace and hobbies. Instead, it felt... confusing.

On day one, she made a celebratory breakfast, sat down with her coffee, and realized something: she had nothing to do. For the first time in forever, no one needed a snack, a bandage, or a pap smear.

Enter: butterflies.

She'd always loved them, specifically, monarchs. As a little girl, she chased them through her backyard in Illinois, naming each one like a dramatic soap opera character (Beatrice the Brave, Felicity the Flighty). Somewhere between the night shifts and math homework and menopause, she forgot all about those winged wonders. Until one fateful scroll through the internet brought her to a site called Monarch Joint Venture. Cue the butterflies... and the clicking.

She found an eco-tour that followed the monarch migration, yes, like actually followed them. From the US to the mystical forests of Michoacán, Mexico. Margaret booked it before she could talk herself out of it, or consult her kids, who would inevitably say things like, "Isn't that dangerous?" and "Do butterflies even know you're there?"

"It's fine," she told them, throwing hiking boots into a suitcase. "I've survived childbirth and fluorescent hospital lighting. I can survive a nature hike."

The adventure began in Texas, tagging and tracking the monarchs, which turned out to be delightfully chaotic. ("I think I just glued a sticker to a leaf!")

She met other nature nerds, some of whom wore matching butterfly earrings unironically, and quickly realized she was among her people.

And then came Michoacán.

She stood in the forest, surrounded by thousands, millions, of monarchs. They clung to trees like vibrant confetti. One landed on her nose. Another had the audacity to poop on her shoulder, and she cried anyway. Because it was stunning. And weird. And exactly what she needed.

Retirement wasn't about winding down. It was about finally following something just for her, something wild, beautiful, and a little unpredictable. Like her.

As the butterflies lifted into the sky, Margaret whispered, "Same, girl. Same."

The Wrap-Up: Your Hobby Doesn't Need to Make Sense, Just Make You Happy

Well, there you have it—proof that retirement hobbies don't have to involve crocheting coasters or alphabetizing spice racks. Whether you're snuggling babies, throwing axes, or becoming the neighborhood's top ghost whisperer, the only rule is this: if it makes you smile, it counts.

You've spent decades doing what was expected. Now? You get to explore what's unexpected. So go ahead, make chocolate that would make Willy Wonka weep. Bedazzle a taxidermy squirrel named Shirley. Fire dance in your backyard (with proper safety precautions, of course!). You're not here to pass the time, you're here to light it up.

And speaking of lighting things up...

Turn the page, because next up you're going to learn how to stop overthinking, start saying yes, and surprise the hell out of yourself. You've got nothing to prove, but so much life left to play with.

Let's go and say yes to some things that make no sense—but make for incredible stories!

CHAPTER 7

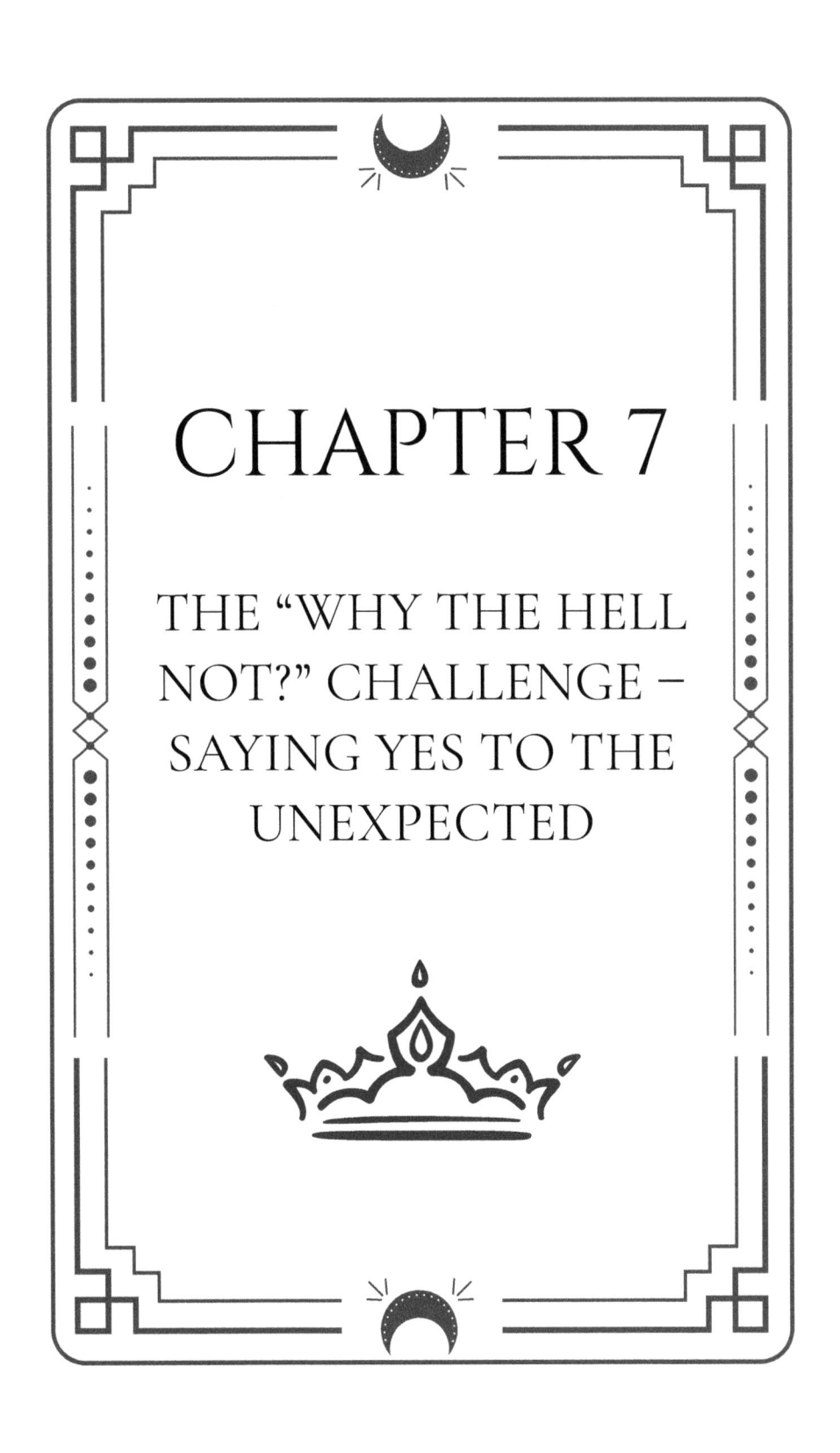

THE "WHY THE HELL NOT?" CHALLENGE – SAYING YES TO THE UNEXPECTED

You've spent decades doing the responsible thing. You've been the one with the calendar, the casserole, the contingency plan. But now? Now it's time to loosen the grip on "should" and start living in the glorious realm of "why the hell not?"

It's time to say yes to things that make no practical sense but sound ridiculously fun. It's not about throwing caution to the wind, it's about throwing routine to the wind. Because you're not here to tiptoe through your golden years. You're here to strut through them in sparkly sneakers, trying things that make your friends say, "Wait, you did what?!"

Whether it's skinny dipping under a full moon, auditioning for a salsa troupe, or ziplining through a jungle while screaming like a teenage boy in a haunted house, this is your moment to say yes to joy, chaos, and adventure. Because honestly... why the hell not?

69

Join a Renaissance Fair as a Performer

Time to Embrace That Inner Pirate or Queen

You've worn a lot of hats in life, but have you ever worn a feathered one while shouting "Huzzah!" at strangers in a muddy field? Joining a Renaissance fair isn't just a hobby, it's a portal. You'll be transformed into a tavern wench, noble lady, pirate captain, or bard, complete with a fake accent, dramatic hand gestures, and so much costume jewelry. You don't need acting experience, just enthusiasm and a willingness to commit to the bit. Fairs across the country are always looking for volunteers, street performers, and character extras. You'll get a script, a character, and a community of delightful weirdos who take their turkey legs very seriously. It's loud, it's weird, and it's an absolute blast. You'll laugh 'til you snort, flirt with knights, and rediscover the part of you that loved playing dress-up. Retirement isn't about fading into the background. It's about grabbing a sword (foam or otherwise) and yelling "To the mead tent!" with pride.

Say Yes to Every Invitation for a Month

See Where Life Takes You When You Stop Saying No

Let's play a little game: For one month, you have to say yes to *every* invitation. Dinner with your neighbor's book club? Yes. Volunteering for a community garden even though you kill succulents? Yes. A moonlit drum circle in a park with strangers named Moonbeam and Carl? Also yes. Why? Because "no" is easy. "Yes" is where the magic lives. The "Yes Month" challenge isn't about being reckless, it's about being open. You might discover a love for pottery. Or a new circle of friends. Or that you actually do enjoy hiking, provided there's wine and cheese at the top. Life opens up when you stop closing it off. Will every yes lead to a life-changing epiphany? Probably not. But every yes is a doorway to something new: laughter, connection, weird stories, and moments that wake you up inside. Say yes, and see where the hell you end up. Spoiler alert: it's going to be fun.

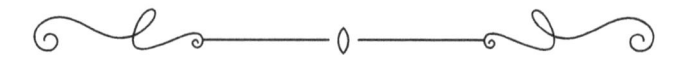

71

SAY YES TO A MYSTERY TRIP
Let the Universe Pick the Playlist

Have you ever heard of Pack Up + Go? It's a surprise travel service that sends you somewhere new in the US but you don't know where until the day you leave. It's like giving your inner wanderlust a glitter bomb. All you do is choose your budget, travel preferences, and how far you're willing to go. Then, boom, an envelope arrives in the mail a few days before your trip. Inside is your destination, itinerary, and a gentle dare to explore with curiosity wide open. Remember, retirement is the perfect time to flirt with spontaneity. You've followed the schedules, made the lunches, showed up to meetings, juggled responsibilities. Now? It's time to let life surprise you for once. Whether you use a service like Pack Up + Go or create your own "spin-the-globe" version with a friend, the real thrill is in letting go. Say yes to the unexpected. Yes to not knowing. Yes to showing up at an airport or train station with nothing but a carry-on and the delicious question, "Where am I going?" Let the universe—and maybe a good travel algorithm—be your concierge!

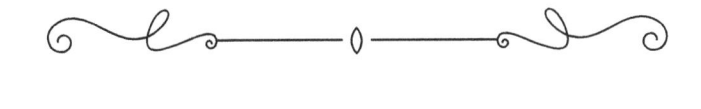

72

Train to Be a Stuntwoman

No, you're probably not going to be leaping from helicopters anytime soon (unless that's your vibe, in which case, respect). But training like a stuntwoman? That's a whole different story, and a total confidence boost. There are actual classes that teach you how to fall safely, fake a punch, stage a fight, and roll out of danger like a boss. Studios like Fight or Flight Academy or local action schools offer intro classes to stunt basics, and let's just say… it's way more fun than Pilates. You'll be surprised at how quickly your body remembers how to move, duck, dive, and sass. You get bonus points for impressing the grandkids and feel like a Marvel character at brunch. Even if you never go pro (or off the porch), you'll walk taller, think quicker, and have one hell of a party story. After all, why ease into retirement when you can roll into it, literally, with a dramatic shoulder tumble and a mock scream? Action heroine energy, unlocked.

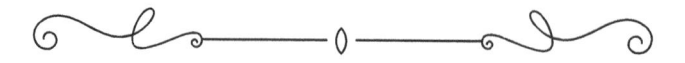

Go on a Date in Every City You Visit Just for the Stories

Who says romance is only for the young and clueless? You're wiser, wittier, and way more interesting than anyone scrolling through dating apps in their 20s. So, next time you travel, try this: one city, one date. No pressure. No expectations. Just you, living your best life and collecting stories worthy of a memoir titled Swiped at Sixty. Apps like Bumble, Hinge, and even old-school Meetup groups can help you connect with interesting locals who are more than happy to show you their city, and maybe their heart. (Or at least their favorite taco place.) Maybe it's coffee with an artist in Asheville, dinner with a surfer in Santa Cruz, or a flamenco show with a philosopher in Madrid. Best-case scenario? Unexpected sparks. Worst-case? You spend an hour with someone mildly weird, then go back to your hotel and eat dessert in bed while texting your friends every juicy detail. Dating isn't just about love. It's about being open to possibility, and maybe getting a little flirty over fondue.

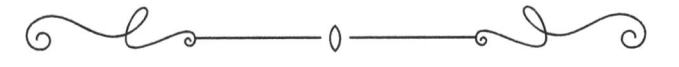

Buy a Last-Minute Plane Ticket to Anywhere

Spin a Globe, Point, and Go

Remember when you used to plan vacations 10 months in advance with printed itineraries and emergency contact lists? Yeah… this is not that. This is chaos travel. Wild, thrilling, possibly-don't-tell-your-family-until-you-land kind of travel. Here's how it works: you find a last-minute flight (try Google Flights, Skyscanner, or Next Vacay), close your eyes, and pick. Maybe it's Portugal. Maybe it's Boise. Maybe it's somewhere you can't pronounce but sounds like an adventure. Throw some clothes in a bag, grab your passport, and go. You'll land somewhere you didn't expect, with no plan other than "say yes and explore." Eat strange snacks. Take confusing public transportation. Get slightly lost. Make friends with a stranger who helps you find your hotel. This isn't about ticking landmarks off a list, it's about reminding yourself that freedom feels like a boarding pass and a heart-pounding with possibility. It's not irresponsible. It's alive. And it might just be the best trip of your life.

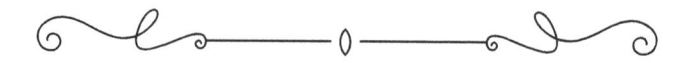

75

Ride in a Hot Air Balloon Over a Place You've Never Been

If retirement had an Instagram moment, this would be it: floating above a stunning landscape in a giant wicker basket, wrapped in a scarf, holding a glass of champagne, grinning like someone who finally figured out how to enjoy life. Hot air balloon rides are whimsical, peaceful, and surprisingly quiet (other than the occasional burst of flame, which, let's be honest, makes you feel slightly like a dragon queen). Whether you're drifting over Napa Valley, the Moroccan desert, or a sleepy countryside town, the view is unmatched, and so is the sense of total freedom. You'll wake up before dawn, bundle up, and watch the balloon inflate like something out of a dream. Then suddenly, you're airborne. The wind becomes your copilot. Your worries? Gone. Your phone signal? Probably also gone, which is a bonus. Most balloon rides end with a champagne toast because, obviously, you just floated in a balloon through the sky. If that's not a reason to celebrate, what is?

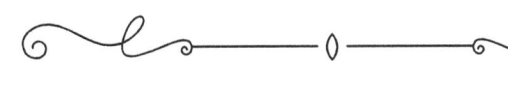

76

Join a Karaoke Contest Even If You Can't Sing

You don't need perfect pitch, you need guts. And maybe some glitter. Karaoke contests are not about talent. They're about commitment. And if you walk up on that stage and give your heart to Whitney Houston or Bon Jovi, people will cheer like you just won *The Voice*. Your job isn't to hit every note. Your job is to feel every note. To dramatically point into the crowd during the chorus. To wink at the bartender mid-verse. To toss in jazz hands even if the song doesn't call for it. You'll be amazed at how empowered you feel once that mic is in your hand and the crowd starts clapping just for showing up. Even if your voice sounds like a cat stuck in a blender, you'll walk off stage to applause, because you dared. And that kind of courage is the real standing ovation. Don't forget, you might actually win and have the best story for brunch.

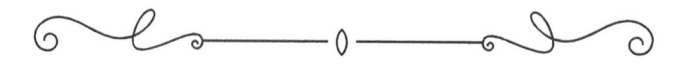

77

Try an Adrenaline-Pumping Sport
Skydiving? Bungee Jumping? Why Not?

If you've ever found yourself saying, "I'm too old for that," it's time to take a seat and hang on tight. Skydiving, bungee jumping, ziplining, paragliding, these adventures aren't just reserved for thrill-seeking twenty-somethings; they're beckoning you too. Yes, you, the one who's already navigated the wild world of toddler tantrums, office politics, and endless group texts with family members. You're practically a superhero! Now, it's time to elevate your game and show off those skills in mid-air. Just make sure to book with a reputable company (seriously, safety first), sign that waiver (try not to overthink it), and take a deep, calming breath. When you finally jump—or fly, or fall, or soar—you'll discover a thrilling truth: you've never felt more alive. Adrenaline has this magical quality of transforming fear from a stop sign into a vibrant green light. And when you finally touch down (legs shaky and a grin plastered across your face), you'll have one unforgettable mic-drop moment. You didn't just dream of living fully; you leapt right into it. Literally.

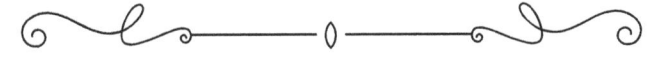

78

Take a Pole Dancing or Burlesque Class Because Confidence Never Retires

If you think pole dancing or burlesque is only for 20-somethings in stilettos, it's time you got acquainted with your new alter ego: Velvet Vixen of the Retirement Renaissance. Pole and burlesque classes are popping up everywhere, and many studios love working with bold, confident women who are trying something totally new. You don't need abs of steel or a performance background. You just need a little curiosity and a willingness to strut awkwardly your first time and laugh your way through it. Pole dancing builds core strength, balance, and sass. Burlesque? That's an art form of humor, glamour, and cheeky empowerment. You'll learn how to walk like you mean it, peel a glove with flair, and own your body in a whole new way. You'll leave class glowing with the kind of confidence that makes you want to wink at yourself in the mirror. Because this isn't about impressing anyone else, it's about falling in love with your bold, sensual, still-got-it self.

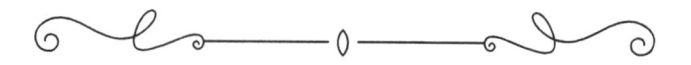

79

Pretend to Be a Tourist in Your Own City for a Day

You've lived in your city for years… decades, even. You know which grocery store has the best bakery and which street has that one pothole that never gets fixed. But have you ever actually explored it? Pretending to be a tourist in your own town is not only fun, it's hilarious. Strap on a fanny pack. Grab a map. Speak in an accent if you're feeling bold. Ask a stranger where "the famous art piece" is and see what happens. Visit the museum you've never stepped into. Take the historical tour you always roll your eyes at. Eat at that kitschy restaurant with the neon flamingo out front. You'll discover things about your city, and yourself, you never knew. It's a reminder that adventure isn't just "out there." It's everywhere. Sometimes you don't need a plane ticket to shake things up. You just need a fresh perspective… and maybe a souvenir snow globe from the gift shop.

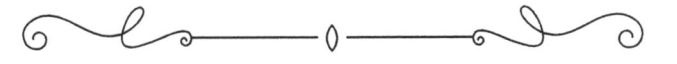

80

Go Skinny Dipping in the Ocean at Night—With or Without a Group of Friends

There's something wildly freeing about running into the ocean in your birthday suit under the moonlight. Maybe it's the fact that no one's watching (hopefully). Maybe it's that you've officially reached the age where shame has packed up and left the building. Either way, skinny dipping at night is a big, bold YES. Bring a few fearless friends, some towels, and a bottle of bubbly, or go solo and make it your little secret. Find a quiet, safe beach, keep an eye on the tide, and prepare for some shrieking (because, let's be honest, the water's never warm). Then… just go for it. You'll feel the rush of rebellion, the thrill of vulnerability, and the joy of not giving a single damn what anyone thinks. It's not about looking good, it's about feeling good. About claiming your freedom, your wildness, and your right to be a little scandalous at any age. Bonus points if you yell "I regret nothing!" while running in.

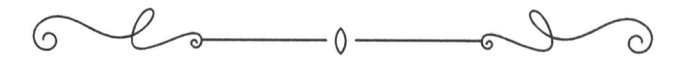

The Bridge, the Bungee, and the Best Friend Who Definitely Didn't Sign Up for This

Six months into retirement, Janice was bored.

Not just "I guess I'll clean out the junk drawer" bored, existentially bored. She'd already tried knitting (gave up halfway through a scarf that looked like it had emotional issues), binged every British crime show on Netflix, and organized her closet drawer so aggressively it was now a shrine to color-coded shoes.

What she wanted, no, *needed*, was a jolt. Something that would make her feel alive, not just "pleasantly napping on the couch."

So she called the only person who would be just crazy enough to consider it.

"Marcy," she said, "pack a bag. We're going to British Columbia."

There was a long pause on the other end. "Is this a winery thing?"

"No," Janice said, practically vibrating with excitement. "We're going bungee jumping."

Marcy choked on her tea.

A week later, the two stood on a rickety-looking platform 150 feet above the Cheakamus River, strapped into harnesses that did not look thick enough to support postmenopausal bravery. Their jump guide, who looked like he moonlighted as a snowboarder and had a man bun you could park a bike in, smiled and said, "Don't worry, ladies. Gravity does all the work."

"Charming," Marcy muttered, eyeing the drop like it had personally insulted her.

Janice, meanwhile, was beaming. "This is it," she whispered. "This is my Eat, Pray, Plunge moment."

"More like Pray, Pee, Panic," Marcy whispered back.

Janice went first. With arms outstretched and a gleeful yell that sounded suspiciously like "Tell my kids I'm fabulous!", she dove off the bridge like she was swan-diving into the second act of her life. She bounced, she flailed, she screamed, she laughed. She came back up breathless, mascara streaked, and completely euphoric.

Then it was Marcy's turn.

"I hate you," she said as they clipped her in.

"I know," Janice replied, grinning.

Marcy screamed the entire way down, a sound that started like terror but morphed into pure, cathartic release. By the time she was hanging upside down over the river, she was cackling.

Later, they sat on a bench, dry underwear, sipping hot chocolate, legs wobbly, adrenaline still surging.

"You do realize we just flung ourselves off a perfectly good bridge," Marcy said.

"Yes," Janice said, "and I've never felt more alive."

They high-fived. Then promised to do something less terrifying next time.

Which, for the record, ended up being indoor skydiving. But that's a whole other story.

The Wrap-Up: You're Not Crazy, You're Courageous

Look at you, saying yes like it's your new superpower. From hot air balloons to pole dancing, axe throwing to impromptu trip-taking, you've proven something big: your best stories might still be waiting on the other side of *Why the hell not?*

You've spent a lifetime being wise, careful, and practical. But now? You've earned the right to be curious, wild, and a little unpredictable. These aren't midlife crises, they're midlife quests. And each "yes" you say rewrites the old, tired script about what retirement is supposed to look like.

But here's the twist: some of those unexpected yeses might light a whole new fire inside you. The kind of fire that doesn't just spark joy, it sparks purpose. Because maybe what you really need next isn't just another adventure... maybe it's a whole new career.

So, turn the page, fearless one, because next up is badass career changes—because you're not done yet. Your resume is about to get *really* interesting.

CHAPTER 8

BADASS CAREER CHANGES– BECAUSE YOU'RE NOT DONE YET

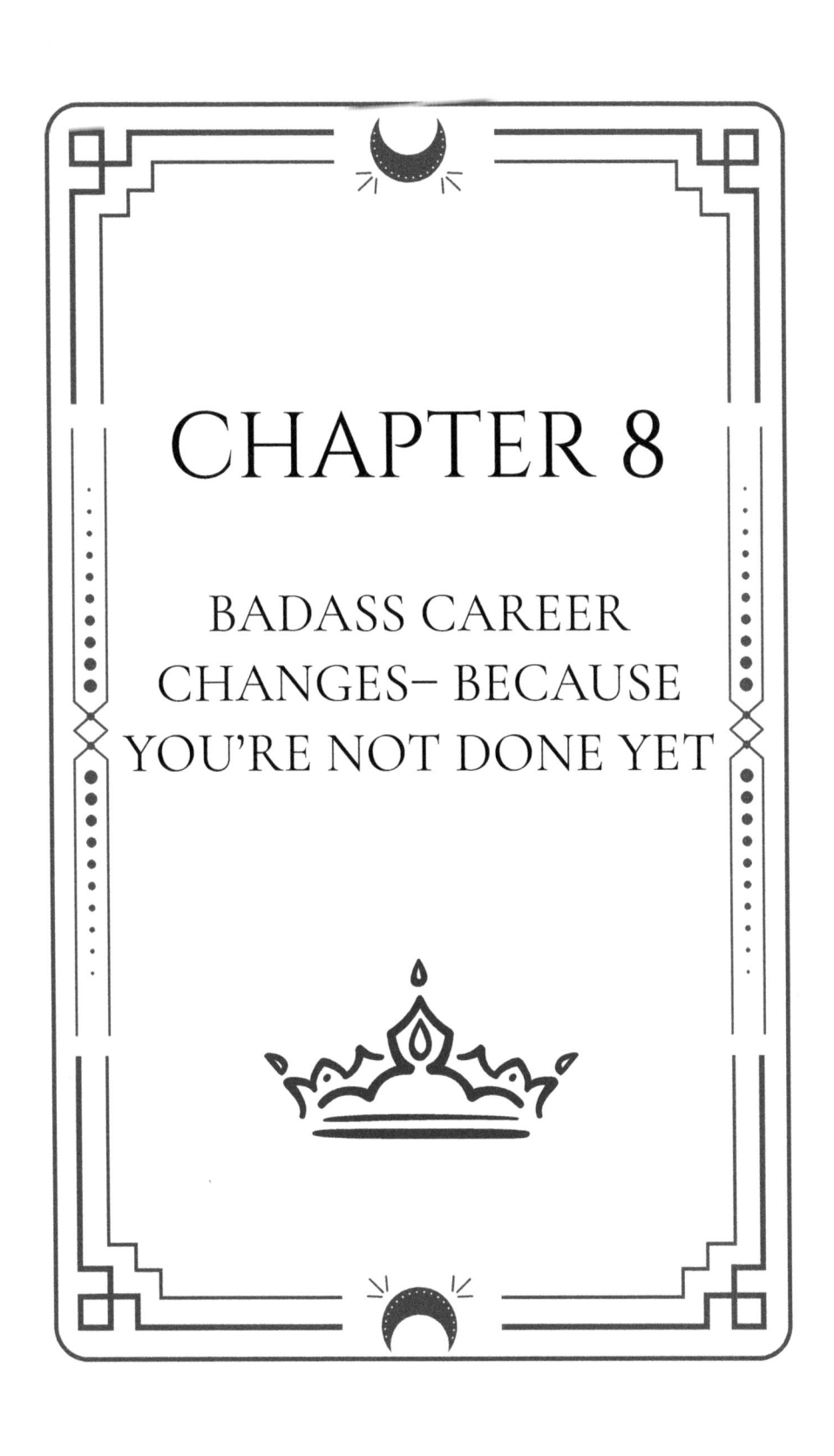

You didn't come this far, survive fluorescent lighting, office potlucks, diaper duty, and decades of emotional labor just to fade into the background and perfect your backswing. No offense to golf, but maybe you've got a few bigger swings to take.

This chapter is your invitation to throw the rulebook out the window, preferably while wearing lipstick and blasting Tina Turner. What if your second act isn't a nap, but a plot twist? What if retirement isn't the end of your career, but the juicy middle part where things get really interesting?

You could start a business, write a novel, become a tour guide, teach belly dancing, or launch a YouTube channel about haunted thrift stores. The job market isn't just for millennials with ring lights anymore, it's for women with grit, wit, and zero tolerance for boring.

Forget "What do you want to do in retirement?" Let's ask the better question: *Who do you want to become next?*

Because you're just getting started.

81

Professional Mermaid

Yes, People Get Paid to Wear a Tail and Swim at Events

If you've ever found yourself immersed in *The Little Mermaid*, daydreaming, *I could totally slay in that tail*, then buckle up because you're about to embark on a new career: professional mermaiding. Believe it or not, it's a legitimate vocation that comes with actual paychecks. Think birthday parties, corporate shindigs, dazzling underwater performances at aquariums, and even cameo appearances in music videos. You'll master the art of swimming with a monofin, develop the ability to hold your breath like a pro, and most importantly, you'll captivate the hearts of children who will swear you just swam in from the great blue yonder. To get started, programs like Mermaid Freedive and PADI Mermaid provide comprehensive training, covering everything from safe underwater performance to breathwork and yes, tail handling (no, seriously, it's essential). By joining this sparkling global community, you'll forge lifelong friendships based on scales, shells, and a shared commitment to fabulousness. And if anyone dares doubt your enchanting new role? Just flick your tail, toss your hair, and confidently declare, "I'm not retired, I'm just fabulously off duty."

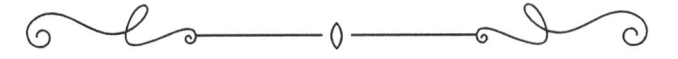

82

Luxury Picnic Planner

Because Instagram-Worthy Outdoor Dining Is Big Business

If you've got a flair for table settings, a Pinterest obsession, and a love of cheese boards so beautiful they belong in a museum, luxury picnic planning might just be your calling. This booming industry is all about creating stunning outdoor dining experiences for clients who want magic without lifting a finger, or a picnic basket. From beach setups with floor pillows and twinkle lights to backyard birthdays with balloon arches and charcuterie for days, you'll get to flex your design muscles and charge handsomely for your creativity. Sites like Picnic Makers or The Picnic Collective show you what's possible, and profitable. Start small: offer services for friends, snap gorgeous photos, and build a social media presence. Before you know it, you'll be the go-to picnic queen in your city, known for setups that say romantic movie scene meets Martha Stewart on rosé. Bonus? You'll never have to eat sad sandwiches on a plaid blanket again.

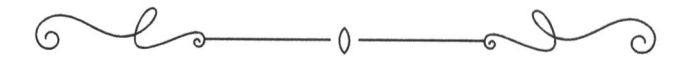

83

Foley Artist (Movie Sound Effects Person)

If You Like Making Weird Noises, This Is for You

Do you get a kick out of crunching gravel beneath your boots? Or maybe you've taken a whack at a head of lettuce just to replicate that satisfying punch sound? Well, congratulations, you might be on the path to becoming a Foley artist! These unsung heroes work behind the scenes to craft the sound effects that bring film, TV, and video games to life. From footsteps to the swoosh of a sword, and even the ominous creak of a door, it's all part of the audio alchemy they perform. Studios are always on the lookout for fresh perspectives and innovative minds, so why not dive in? You can find online courses like Pro Sound Effects and FilmSound.org to get you started, teaching you the ins and outs of creating spine-tingling audio. And don't worry about the setup, turn your garage into a mini sound studio filled with quirky props like celery, metal sheets, and rubber gloves (you'll understand soon enough!). If being a little eccentric sounds appealing, you could turn this passion into a money-making venture that feels more like play than work!

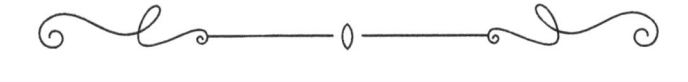

84

PET PSYCHIC

Are You Sure Fluffy Doesn't Have Something Important to Say?

Your cat stares at walls. Your dog sighs dramatically. And your grand-pug definitely has trust issues. What if… they're trying to *tell* you something? Welcome to the wild, wonderful world of pet communication. Pet psychics (or animal intuitives, if you want the fancier title) claim to tap into the thoughts, feelings, and mysterious needs of our furry companions. Whether you believe in it or just want to lean into the vibe, there's a real market for this. You can train through programs like Danielle MacKinnon's Soul Level Animal Communication or the Animal Energy Certification. Clients will pay good money to know why Fluffy won't stop licking the furniture or if Baxter is holding a grudge over the groomer incident of 2019. You'll laugh. You might cry. And even if you don't end up Dr. Dolittle-ing your way to fame, you'll connect deeply with animals and their humans. Don't forget, pets are way easier clients than humans. No Yelp reviews.

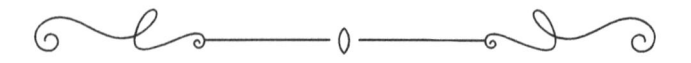

85

VOICEOVER ACTOR FOR CARTOONS AND VIDEO GAMES

Get Paid to Be Animated

Do people tell you your voice belongs on the radio? Have you ever read a bedtime story with accents and dramatic flair? Then it might be time to become a voiceover actor and no, you don't have to move to Hollywood. From quirky cartoon characters to epic video game heroes to training videos for mildly terrifying HR modules, the world needs voice talent—especially voices with warmth, wisdom, and personality, just like you. Check out sites like Voices.com, Edge Studio, and Gravy for the Brain that can help you learn, record demos, and start booking gigs. All you need is a decent mic, a quiet closet (hello, home studio), and the courage to let loose and get a little ridiculous. The best part? You can work in pajamas, make weird noises, and get paid for having fun. If retirement is your time to find your *true* voice, why not make it your job, too?

86

Bounty Hunter (Yes, Really!)
Channel Your Inner Action Hero

No, this isn't just a gig reserved for guys named Chet sporting goatees and mirrored sunglasses. You, yes, fabulous retired woman, can legally step into the adrenaline-fueled world of bounty hunting (aka fugitive recovery agent), where tracking down bail-jumpers turns into a cash-collecting adventure. Imagine it: part detective work, part heart-racing excitement, and a dash of "Is this even real life?" You'll need to dive into training courses, so don't forget to check your state's requirements! A great starting point is the National Association of Fugitive Recovery Agents, which offers valuable resources. You'll master self-defense, surveillance techniques, and the art of outsmarting folks who are great at playing hide-and-seek. Yes, it is totally possible that your kids may think you've gone off the deep end, but they have no idea how thrilling it feels to declare, "I can't chat right now, I'm chasing down a guy with unpaid bail in a Waffle House parking lot." Welcome to your new retirement hobby: delivering justice while sporting leather jackets with flair!

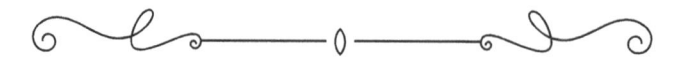

87

GET CERTIFIED AS A WILDERNESS SURVIVAL EXPERT – LEARN HOW TO LIVE OFF THE GRID

Sure, you've survived board meetings, toddler tantrums, and holiday dinners with your sister-in-law, but could you start a fire with a stick and sheer willpower? Wilderness survival certification says, "Yes, I can, and I brought snacks." Becoming a certified survival expert means learning to build shelter, purify water, track animals (or your lost phone), and basically thrive like a forest goddess in hiking boots. Courses from places like Boulder Outdoor Survival School or NOLS will teach you the skills you hope you'll never need, but feel *super cool* knowing you have. Plus, you'll develop a whole new appreciation for duct tape and pine needles. You'll also intimidate everyone at backyard barbecues when you casually drop, "That reminds me of the time I made a hammock out of paracord and inner peace." And hey, it's always good to know how to survive in the wild—especially if someone forgets the Wi-Fi password again!

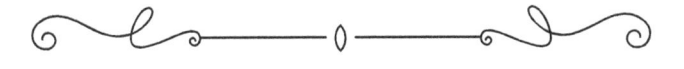

88

PROFESSIONAL BRIDESMAID

Yes, You Get Paid to Be in Weddings

If you love weddings but hate the drama of actually knowing the bride, you're in luck. Enter: professional bridesmaid, a very real, very fabulous job where you're hired to stand by a stranger's side, wrangle groomsmen, calm nervous in-laws, and look great doing it. Companies like Bridesmaid for Hire pioneered this role, proving that sometimes, people don't want to burden their flaky college roommate with responsibility, but they do want someone reliable, charming, and emotionally unflappable. That's where you come in. You'll learn to bustle dresses, fix makeup with a Q-tip, write last-minute toasts, and hold a bouquet like a pro. Some gigs are emotional support, others are full-on logistical command centers. Either way, you'll leave with a goodie bag and a great story. And when guests ask how you know the bride? Just smile mysteriously and say, "Oh, I'm a professional." Then sip your champagne like the boss you are.

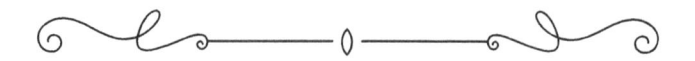

89

Train as an Astronomer and Host Stargazing Events

If you've always felt a little starry-eyed and not just after two glasses of wine, then it might be time to look up, literally. Amateur astronomy is the gateway to a universe of discovery, and yes, you can turn it into an actual business. You can get trained through programs like Sky & Telescope's Astronomy for Beginners or The Astronomical League, and before you know it, you'll know your Betelgeuse from your black holes. With a quality telescope and a little charisma, you can host your own stargazing events. Think backyard astronomy parties, date nights under the stars, or guided celestial tours in national parks. People love a knowledgeable guide who can point out planets and drop cool facts like, "That star exploded a million years ago, and now you're seeing its ghost." You'll reconnect with the mystery and magic of the universe, and become that enchanting, slightly mystical woman who always knows when Mercury is in retrograde. Spoiler: it probably is.

90

Run a Goat Yoga Retreat
It's Yoga With Goats. Enough Said!

Absolutely, goat yoga is a thing, and no, you certainly don't need a chiseled physique or a countryside backdrop to get started! Goat yoga is just what it sounds like: picture yourself in downward dog, inhaling that fresh air, while tiny goats frolic on your back, adding an extra layer of fun to your zen moment. It's a mix of laughter and warmth, and let's be honest, it's super Instagrammable! Begin by collaborating with a local farm or consider adopting a few friendly goats of your own. To kick things off, enroll in a basic yoga instructor course (check out Yoga Alliance for solid options). After that, you can organize charming pop-up classes in parks or spacious fields. Want to take it up a notch? Include some delightful snacks and soothing herbal tea, creating a complete goat wellness experience. Trust me, people will flock to your sessions, ready to do yoga they might not fully grasp, all while adoring those adorable goats. Get ready for some serious giggles—who knew working out could be this entertaining? And yes, goats do their business; just roll with it, it's all part of the charm! Your new entrepreneurial mantra? "Stretch. Breathe. Goat."

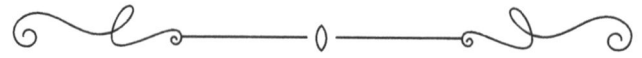

91

Learn Hypnosis and Past Life Regression Therapy

Explore the Mind

You've always suspected your intuition was strong. You've probably said things like, "I have a feeling…" or "You just have that energy…" Well, now it's time to level up and use those instincts to help others explore their subconscious, unlock stuck patterns, or discover whether they were Cleopatra in a past life. Hypnotherapy and past life regression are in-demand services for people looking for healing, clarity, and fascinating inner journeys. You can train and get certified through reputable programs like the Hypnosis Motivation Institute or The Newton Institute for past life regression. It's deep, it's trippy, and it's incredibly rewarding. Imagine guiding someone through their fears… or helping them discover they were once a Viking blacksmith with commitment issues. It's like being a therapist, a detective, and a spiritual tour guide, without needing a PhD. You can use the skills to finally understand why you always tear up during car commercials and feel irrationally drawn to medieval armor.

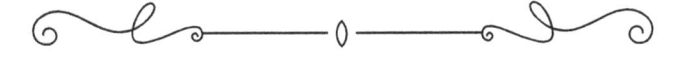

The Voice in Her Head—And Every Kid's Bedtime Story

Debbie had tried everything.

Since retiring, she'd attempted pottery (all her mugs looked like sad hats), took a French cooking class (burned the béchamel, made peace with takeout), and even joined a gardening club before realizing she was more "plastic succulents and sarcasm" than "organic kale and compost tea."

She wasn't outdoorsy. She wasn't crafty. She wasn't going to pickle things. What she *was*, however, was loud, dramatic, and absolutely *magnetic* when she read to her grandkids.

"Grammy! Do the squirrel voice again!" they'd yell.

"Only if you behave," she'd say, then launch into a high-pitched chipmunk with a questionable British accent. It was her thing. She gave every character a voice, every story a performance. Her daughter once said, "You sound like a cartoon. In the best possible way."

And that was it.

Debbie had found her thing.

She started small, recording samples in her closet between coats and an old George Foreman grill. She took a free online workshop through Voices.com, learned how to edit her audio ("Why is my nose so loud?!"), and invested in a mic that looked like it could launch a space mission.

Soon, she was auditioning for children's audiobook gigs, and landing them. One book turned into five. Five turned into a whole series about a hedgehog with anxiety and a raccoon who sang opera. Debbie made each voice a full production, sometimes startling her husband mid-laundry with a sudden "Narrator mode: On."

Her grandkids? Ecstatic. Her neighbors? Confused by the pirate shouting from her guest room. Her retirement? Officially upgraded to delightfully dramatic.

She didn't need a garden. She had a studio.

She didn't need hiking boots. She had headphones.

And every time a new story landed in her inbox, she'd smile, clear her throat, and say, "Alright, my little listeners. Are you ready for an adventure?"

Because Grammy had finally found her hobby, and it had a very tiny fanbase with sticky fingers and wild imaginations.

The Wrap-Up: Your Second Act Deserves a Better Job Title

Isn't it fantastic, exploring careers that don't just pay the bills, but light you up like a birthday cake on fire? Whether you're wearing a mermaid tail, wrangling goats, or starting your own bridesmaid empire, you've proven one undeniable truth: Retirement isn't the end of your work life, it's the beginning of your dream life.

Gone are the days of staying in your lane, playing it safe, or wondering if you're "too old" to start something new. You're not too old; you're too seasoned to not do what you love.

So go ahead, try something outrageous. Start something from scratch. Laugh in the face of LinkedIn and say, "I'm building my own resume now, thanks."

Whether it's cosmic, chaotic, or just slightly absurd, your next career chapter is all about joy, freedom, and not asking for anyone's approval.

But once you've launched your mermaid-wedding-goat-yoga empire... you deserve a vacation.

Turn the page, because next up is how to travel without children and enjoy it, where you finally get to plan a trip that doesn't involve nap schedules, Goldfish crackers, or 17 bathroom stops. This time, the only person you're packing for is you. Let's go.

CHAPTER 9

HOW TO TRAVEL WITHOUT CHILDREN AND ENJOY IT

Remember when travel meant juggling Fruit Roll-Ups, emergency crayons, and a child screaming "I don't like this plane!" at full volume? Yeah... that version of travel retired when you did.

Welcome to your new jet-set era, where you pack for yourself, sip wine at the gate instead of wiping applesauce off your pants, and actually get to sleep on the flight (cue angelic choir). This chapter is all about reclaiming travel on your terms: spontaneous detours, long breakfasts, no theme parks (unless you want to go!), and zero judgment if your suitcase is filled with caftans and good snacks. No more being the family cruise director. No more researching "kid-friendly restaurants" in five different time zones. Now, you travel light—emotionally and literally—and focus on things like pleasure, freedom, and finally using your damn passport for something exciting.

Let's book the trip, ditch the itinerary, and start seeing the world with fresh eyes and fabulous shoes. Because you're not just taking a vacation, you're taking yourself somewhere spectacular.

92

Take a "James Bond" Trip: Stay in Luxury Hotels, Drink Martinis, and Gamble in Monte Carlo

You've absolutely earned your Bond moment, and no, we're not referring to the brooding Sean Connery kind. We're talking about fully embracing your glamorous espionage fantasy without the risk of actual bullets flying your way. Consider booking a swanky suite at the Hôtel de Paris in Monte Carlo, and if you don't own a yacht, just sweet-talk someone who does. Order that dry martini with unapologetic style, then saunter into the casino as if you're carrying both state secrets and a diamond tiara. And let's be honest: You might as well wear something slinky and audacious, even if your chips vanish faster than a classic Aston Martin in a high-speed chase. This isn't a trip designed for those on a budget; this is a "why the heck not?" escapade. You're not evading any villains; you're sprinting toward a ridiculously fabulous time. And when someone addresses you as "madame," flash a knowing smile because you just might be holding the keys to the world's best-kept secrets in your designer clutch. For an unforgettable experience, check out travel deals on sites like Booking.com or Airbnb for luxe stays, and grab your martini recipe off YouTube to perfect your mixology!

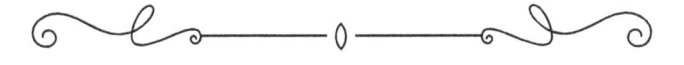

93

Spend a Night in an Igloo in Finland

Sleep Under the Northern Lights

Forget about five-star hotels, let's talk about a night that's truly out of this world! Picture yourself beneath the stars in Finland, where you can stay in a glass-roofed igloo and witness the Northern Lights waltzing above you like nature's own spectacular performance. It's akin to sleeping inside a snow globe, only now you can enjoy heated floors and, thankfully, proper indoor plumbing. Check out the Kakslauttanen Arctic Resort, where cozy glass domes await, perfect for enjoying reindeer safaris and saying nonchalantly, "Oh, I just spent some time in the Arctic Circle last winter, no big deal." You might find yourself donning thermal underwear and your eyelashes could temporarily freeze, but trust me, the first time those radiant lights cascade across the sky will bring genuine tears of joy. This isn't just any getaway; it's a bucket list adventure that feels like stepping straight into a fairytale *and waking up to breakfast in bed*. So, pack your bags and prepare to be awed!

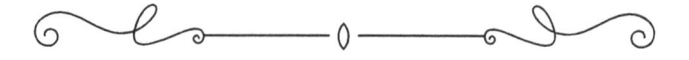

94

TRAIN AS A SAFARI GUIDE IN AFRICA
Who Says You Can't Be an Expert on Lions at 65?

Looking for a retirement story that leaves your neighborhood book club in the dust? Here's a gem: "Oh, I spent last spring tracking lions in Botswana." That's right! You can train as a safari guide with programs like EcoTraining, and let me tell you, it's not just for those fresh-faced 20-somethings in their zip-off pants. This adventure is perfect for bold, inquisitive, and downright *fascinating* women ready to decode the mysteries of the wild—yes, understanding animal scat is on the syllabus! You'll learn to read the bush like it's an epic novel and impress everyone with your newfound bird-call recognition skills. Picture this: cozy campfires, awakening to the gentle sun rising over the savanna, and achieving a deeper connection to the Earth than what any spa can offer. Trust me, once you drop casually into conversation, "Oh, that lioness? She's just protecting her cubs. Totally normal," you won't just have a new story; you'll have changed how everyone sees you forever! So, why not say goodbye to the ordinary and embrace the extraordinary?

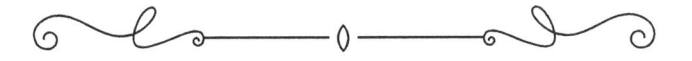

Rent a Private Island

It's Way Less Than You Think

Renting a private island may sound like an indulgence fit only for the ultra-wealthy with their exotic pets, but thanks to platforms like Airbnb and Vladi Private Islands, it could be more attainable than you think. Yes, you heard that right! You can find luxurious getaways for as little as $500 a night, and when you divide that among friends, those dreamy visions of your own slice of paradise become shockingly realistic. Picture yourself snorkeling in crystal-clear waters, sipping cocktails adorned with tiny umbrellas, and playfully exclaiming things like "Release the doves!" for no actual reason. It's a kid-free zone, away from the hustle and bustle, just you, the sun, the sand, and the undeniable ability to saunter down the beach like you've just stepped off a yacht. Don your largest sunhat, the tiniest swimsuit, and don't forget that fabulously gaudy beach novel. This is your time to shine! Because there's nothing quite like sending a cheeky group text saying, "Hey ladies, I'll be on my private island this week. Don't wait up!"

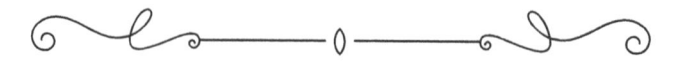

96

DO A MYSTERY TRIP

Let a Travel Agency Plan Everything Without Telling You Where You're Going

Ready to hand over the reins and savor the adventure? It's time to book a mystery trip! Companies like Pack Up + Go and Magical Mystery Tours take care of all the details, keeping your destination under wraps until it's time to board. Picture this: you receive a weather forecast, a vague packing guide, and then, *boom*—you find yourself holding a plane ticket to an undisclosed location. Is it a vineyard getaway? A frosty retreat in Iceland? Or perhaps a swanky train ride through the Rockies? The real excitement lies in the unpredictability. This is the perfect escape for those who've spent a lifetime organizing every family vacation since 1987. Now, it's your turn to be delightfully unprepared. Adventure awaits without the stress of planning! Embrace the joy of spontaneity, and let go of all that control. Trust me, you'll find that surrendering feels downright exhilarating. So kick back, relax, and get ready for a surprise that could change everything. You deserve this thrill!

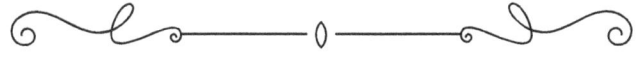

97

LIVE IN A TREEHOUSE AIRBNB IN COSTA RICA

Your childhood dreams of treehouse living just received a fabulous makeover! Costa Rica is bursting with enchanting treehouse Airbnbs. You could be waking up to spectacular rainforest views, enjoying open-air showers, and maybe waving hello to a cheeky monkey or two. Picture sipping your morning coffee while perched high above the clouds, embracing your inner jungle monarch with Wi-Fi access, of course. You can explore magical options like the Treehouse Lodge or sift through Airbnb's "unique stays" section, where you're bound to find your perfect hideaway. Plus, you'll have the ultimate conversation starter: "Oh, I spent some time living in a treehouse in the jungle." How casually cool is that? It's like camping but with a touch of luxury. And fear not, no awkward ladder maneuvers in the dark; these charming retreats come equipped with sturdy stairs and ambiance-setting mood lighting. So, get ready to indulge in an unforgettable experience, where childhood fantasies meet modern comfort in the heart of nature!

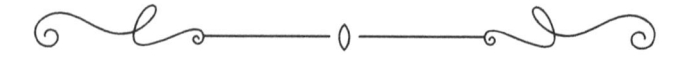

98

WALK WITH WOLVES AT A WILDLIFE SANCTUARY

Connect With the Wild Side of You

If elephants aren't your thing, or you've already crossed "trunk hugs" off your list, how about something a little more... howl-worthy? Picture yourself in the forest, walking side by side with a real, live wolf. Not a zoo wolf. A rescued, rehabilitated, fur-so-thick-you-want-to-dive-in kind of wolf. Places like Mission: Wolf in Colorado or Wolf Connection in California offer educational programs and volunteer opportunities where you can learn about wolf conservation, help care for these majestic creatures, and even walk beside them in a safe, respectful, and completely unforgettable way. You'll learn pack dynamics (kind of like family reunions, but with more howling), deepen your connection with nature, and maybe rediscover a little wildness in yourself, too. It's not about taming the wild. It's about honoring it. And when you get back home and someone asks how retirement's going, you can say, "Oh, you know... just spent the weekend bonding with wolves in the mountains. Totally normal." Because why just find yourself, when you can run with the pack?

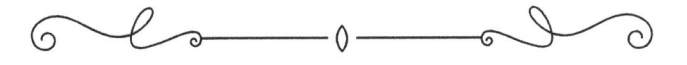

99

SPEND A YEAR LEARNING INDIGENOUS WISDOM FROM DIFFERENT TRIBES

Gain Deep Cultural Insights

This is travel redefined. If you're yearning for a deeper connection and a fresh perspective on the world, dive into a cultural immersion program. Organizations like the Pachamama Alliance and the School for International Training (SIT) provide travel experiences steeped in Indigenous wisdom, sustainability, and spiritual growth. Imagine learning sacred traditions, participating in vibrant ceremonies, and truly honing your listening skills. You'll discover the immense wisdom found in moments of stillness and the restorative power of stepping away from the noise of everyday life. This journey transcends mere tourism; it invites you to become a student of the earth and its inhabitants. Experience life one ceremonial cup of tea at a time. Plus, the bonus? You'll return home transformed, perhaps with a collection of stunning woven scarves that you'll proudly proclaim as your new *ritual garments*. So, pack your bags, leave your expectations behind, and get ready for an adventure that nourishes the soul and sparks your curiosity like never before.

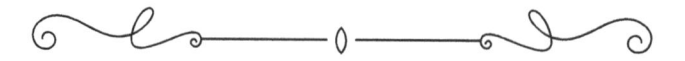

100

Visit Every U.S. National Park
A Nature Bucket List Challenge

Feeling adventurous? How about taking on the ultimate challenge: visiting all 63 U.S. National Parks! Yep, that's right, 63 diverse, breathtaking, and quirky pieces of America waiting for you to explore. Picture massive mountains, sprawling deserts, mysterious swamps, enchanting caves, and even a park made up mainly of volcanic islands. Grab yourself a National Parks Passport and start collecting those stamps like an intrepid explorer. You'll be hiking, sure, but don't forget the boating, stargazing, and indulging in those steamy hot springs, all while munching on more trail mix than you ever thought feasible. Along the way, you'll encounter knowledgeable park rangers who are a treasure trove of information, witness jaw-dropping landscapes, and snap selfies that will make your grandkids green with envy. This isn't just another checklist; it's a bucket list journey in sturdy boots. When friends ask how you spent your retirement, you can proudly share tales of your epic adventure across 63 national parks, solidifying your status as a nature-loving legend. Adventure awaits, so lace up those hiking boots and hit the trail!

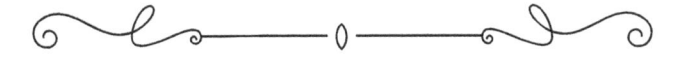

101

Create a House Swap Network for Retirees

Travel Affordably

Are hotel prices putting a damper on your travel dreams? Say goodbye to unexpected costs and towel fees. It's time to kickstart your very own house swap network, targeting fabulous, reliable retirees eager for some adventure without the hefty price tag. You can keep it casual and simply team up with friends, or elevate your game by utilizing platforms like HomeExchange or People Like Us. Here's the concept: I get to soak up the sun in your beach house, and you chill in my cozy mountain cabin. Voilà! A free vacation! Think of it like Airbnb but with a touch more class and a lot fewer lurking socks under the bed. Just add a delightful wine welcome basket, and you have a thriving community of retired women who travel smart and live large. With this network, you're not just exchanging homes; you're creating friendships and experiences that make retirement truly spectacular. So, pack your bags and let the adventures begin!

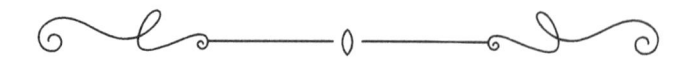

102

Start a Nomadic Learning Group
Travel and Learn With Like-Minded Women

You've mastered the art of flying solo. Now, it's time to gather your squad! A nomadic learning group is a vibrant tribe of curious, open-hearted women who journey together to explore the world while feeding their minds. Picture this: each adventure revolves around a unique topic. Imagine sipping fine Chianti in Tuscany while learning Italian, embracing tranquility in Kyoto with Zen practices and calligraphy, or experiencing healing and altitude-induced epiphanies in Peru. Whether you want to lead your own expedition, join an established group, or start from scratch, the possibilities are endless. Programs like Road Scholar and Wanderful offer fantastic opportunities to connect with like-minded women. This is more than just friendship; it's a delightful blend of education and adventure, wrapped in a suitcase and garnished with room service. Remember, travel isn't just about escaping reality; it's about expanding your horizons and enriching your life with new experiences and friendships that last a lifetime!

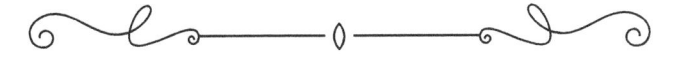

103

Plan the Girls Trip That's Been Postponed for Far Too Long

Eat Pray Love, Anyone?

Let's dive into that epic getaway sitting in your group chat for *seven years* now. You know, the one filled with half-formed ideas, the classic "Ugh, we really need to do this" moments, and a lot of wishful thinking? Well, it's time to shake things up—now is the moment! Book that villa. Select your dream destination. Embrace the delightful chaos! Whether you're craving a tranquil spa retreat in Sedona, twirling forkfuls of pasta in Positano, or hitting the dance floor in Dublin, remember: it's not just about the place. It's about the laughter echoing in the air, the late-night soul-baring chats, and the luxurious freedom of not having to arrange a babysitter anymore. This trip isn't a mere escape from reality; it's a jubilant celebration of friendship, independence, and finally having every reason to go. And yes, you can definitely channel your inner Eat Pray Love diva in those trusty stretchy pants. Just maybe leave the brooding poet behind. Or, hey, if he insists, why not?

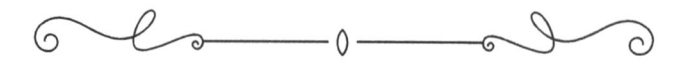

The Wrap-Up: Pack Light, Travel Boldly, and Don't Wait for Permission

There you have it—proof that travel without children doesn't mean loneliness. What it actually means? Liberation. No more emergency snack bags, no more *Dora the Explorer* reruns in hotel rooms, and definitely no more apologizing to strangers on airplanes. This is your time. Your passport. Your adventure.

Whether you're sleeping in igloos, feeding elephants, sipping martinis in Monte Carlo, or just finally taking that long-overdue girls' trip, every journey is a reminder that you're not slowing down. You're leveling up.

So go. Wander. Detour. Book the window seat. Order dessert first. Wear the caftan. Life's too short for boring travel and too long to wait for someone else to say it's okay.

But what's next, you ask?

Oh, just a little something called *The Royal Planner*.

Think of it as your crowning jewel. A downloadable bonus filled with:

- ◊ **12 mini-adventures:** One bold challenge per month to keep the sparkle alive.

- ◊ **Monthly checklists:** Fun, practical ways to actually *do* the things in this book.

- ◊ **A notes section:** For scribbling thoughts, wins, mishaps, and stories worth retelling.

- ◊ **Goals and rewards:** Because every queen deserves a treat for being brave and brilliant.

Let's turn your retirement from something that just happened… into something you're freaking proud of.

Grab your crown. We've got planning to do.

SCAN TO CLAIM YOUR
ROYAL PLANNER

ROYAL BONUS

CONCLUSION

LONG LIVE THE QUEEN
(THAT'S YOU)

Well, we've officially journeyed through 103 fearless, bucket-list-filling, sometimes-sassy, always-adventurous ways to reclaim retirement and reign like the glorious, wise, wildly unstoppable woman you are.

This book wasn't just a list of activities. It was a nudge. A wink. A reminder that this next chapter? It's not a quiet epilogue. It's a whole new volume, and you get to write it in whatever font and color you please.

It's time to remember that retirement is your time to explore, rediscover, and fall in love with new passions. The dreams you set aside while juggling careers, caretaking, and chaos? They're still waiting.

Forget the outdated image of retirement as quiet and beige. You're here to rewrite the script. Wear the leopard print. Launch the podcast. Start the business. This chapter of your life belongs to you, not society's expectations.

Whether it's through girls' trips, nomadic learning circles, or joining a goat yoga tribe (yes, it's still funny), the joy of this moment in your life is meant to be shared. Connection is your secret fuel.

Some of your best moments ahead will come from unplanned detours, surprise yeses, and spontaneous leaps into something slightly terrifying but undeniably thrilling. Let those sparks fly.

So, go ahead. Pick your next big (or small-but-mighty) adventure. Try one thing from this book. Then try another. Then keep going until your grandkids can't keep up with you.

Because this is not the wind-down phase. This is the wake-up call to your most joy-fueled, self-defined, unapologetically bold chapter yet.

And if you loved this book, if it made you laugh, dream, plan, or say, "Oh hell yes!"—please take a moment to leave a review. Your voice helps other fabulous women find the spark they've been looking for too.

If you know an incredible man ready to take on his own legendary retirement, be sure to send him over to check out our companion guide: 103 Fun Ways to Enjoy Retirement Like a King.

Here's to the dreams you've yet to chase, the laughter you've yet to roar, and the adventures that are yours and yours alone.

Now go reign, and don't forget to pack snacks because royalty still gets hungry!

REFERENCES

This book was inspired by a spirit of adventure, creativity, and rebellion. Some ideas and examples mentioned were drawn from publicly available resources, including:

- Mural Arts Program – www.muralarts.org
- Flash Mob America – www.flashmobamerica.com
- MasterClass (Courses by Penn & Teller, Phil Ivey, and more) – www.masterclass.com
- SailAway – www.sailaway.co
- Workaway Cultural Exchange – www.workaway.info
- Archaeological Institute of America – www.archaeological.org

◊   Women's Flat Track Derby Association – www.wftda.com

◊   Volunteer World – www.volunteerworld.com

All trademarks, program names, and organization names are the property of their respective owners and are used here for illustrative and educational purposes only.